PRAISE FOR *LIVING THE RV LIFE*

"If you are considering full-time RVing (and even if you're not), the words *ultimate guide* absolutely describe this book. It is remarkably comprehensive, breezily written, accurate, honest, and inspiring. Marc and Julie have captured the true essence of the RV experience gained from firsthand knowledge. I can't think of a better way to start your next life journey than first traveling through this book with the Bennetts as your copilots."

—Don Cohen, founder and editor-at-large of WinnebagoLife.com

"No one is more passionate about the RV lifestyle than the Bennetts, who have long been driven by a desire to share what they've learned. This book contains essential information for anyone contemplating a transition to RV life."

—John Johnston, associate editor of *Family RVing* magazine, the official publication of the Family Motor Coach Association

"The RV lifestyle is enticing, but the thought of hitting the road in an RV can be overwhelming for even the most adventurous spirit. That's where Marc and Julie's book really helps. There's no substitute for personal experience, but *Living the RV Life* is loaded with insight and information from two people who've 'been there, done that.' It tackles not only the nuts and bolts of RVing but includes the emotional aspect of leaving it all behind and how you can make new friends out on the road. Whether you're a weekend warrior or a full-time RVer, *Living the RV Life* is an easy-to-understand road map for navigating the rough patches and successfully enjoying the RV lifestyle."

—Rick Kessler, managing editor of *RVBusiness*

"Hitting the road in an RV is stressful enough but imagine doing it permanently! Marc and Julie have written the full-time RV opus providing an informative, detailed, and inspirational guide for dreamers and realists alike. If RV living is even a remote possibility in your life, this is the single best place to start that journey."

—Mark Koep, founder and CEO of CampgroundViews.com

"What an excellent resource for anyone looking to transition into or learn more about the RVing lifestyle! Marc and Julie share their knowledge on a wide array of topics, from the basics of RVing and how to keep in touch with people on the road, all the way to how to plan your trips and where to stay. You'll be amazed by the amount of detail in this book, and by the time you're finished, you'll be ready to hit the open road!"

—Melanie Carr, vice president of Escapees RV Club

"We learned most of what we know about RVing the hard way... by trial and error. If we'd had a resource like Marc and Julie when we started RVing, we'd surely have avoided a lot of those early headaches. Now, after more than fifteen years of full-timing, we sure do recognize good RVing advice when we see it. Marc and Julie are a wealth of knowledge, skilled at relating it, and incredibly generous in their efforts to help others avoid the early mistakes so many of us made. Their guide is a great way to learn if RVing is right for you, and get off to a smarter start."

—Peter & John of TheRVgeeks.com

"Marc and Julie Bennett's passion and expertise will help you explore and navigate the fascinating and always exciting world of RVing. *Living the RV Life* is a remarkably complete and well-constructed guide—it's the best copilot you could have as you get ready to hit the road!"

—Curtis Coleman, founder of RVillage.com

"Julie and Marc share their experiences as full-time RVers with passion and enthusiasm, answering most of the common questions and concerns many of us longtimers constantly field. We're thrilled to see a modern book of this caliber hit the shelves so we can refer folks to a solid resource written for those approaching the RV lifestyle, regardless of their age or background."

—Cherie Ve Ard & Chris Dunphy of Technomadia.com

PRAISE FOR *LIVING THE RV LIFE*

"A comprehensive guide for those considering the RV lifestyle. If you're feeling sick, you want a qualified doctor. If you're feeling hungry, you want a real chef. And if you're interested in the RV lifestyle, you want the Bennetts. Not only do Marc and Julie live the RV lifestyle on a daily basis but they write a great book too. They cover everything you want to know—as well as everything you *need to know*—to live life on the road. Highly recommended."

—John Toffler, editor of RVReviews.net

"As a former full-time RVer and current full-time member of the RV industry, I know the lifestyle comes with a learning curve. This book has all of the answers and more, and I can't think of anyone better suited to share this knowledge than Marc and Julie Bennett. There's nothing quite like the freedom of the open road. Hit the pavement with confidence—and keep this book in your glove compartment."

—Jeff Shelton, owner of Wholesale Warranties

"A home run! Marc and Julie will help put your dreams on a fast track and inspire you to explore the possibilities of living a richer and more meaningful life. An honest must-read for all RV enthusiasts and anyone considering the RV lifestyle. This book will get you well on your way."

—Alan Warren of *The RV Show USA*

"A one-stop shop for everything you need to know to get started in the RV life. A riveting read that should be on every RVer's table. Marc and Julie are largely considered preeminent voices of expertise in the RV community. This consideration comes to life with brilliance through the words, visuals, and teachings they've shared with us all through this book. It is without question the most important and helpful blueprint for RVers available today!"

—Eric Odom, producer of the *RV Nomads* movie

"Warning: this book will bring out your inner RVer; it could change your life forever. If you want to learn from the best, dive in and get some *RVLove*. Marc and Julie are true veterans of the road; they show us how to make full-time RVing possible. Hands down the best RV lifestyle book ever published."

—Sean Nichols, COO of Battle Born Batteries

"Working with Marc and Julie over the past few years has been such a pleasure. It's inspiring to follow their story and witness their evolution from interested RVers to full-blown RVing experts. They embody the RV lifestyle, and their stories give others the knowledge and courage to take the next step and embrace the adventure that is life on the road."

—Mary Willkom, public relations/communications manager of Lippert Components

"Julie and Marc have created the ultimate guide for anyone wanting to lead an unconventional and meaningful life on the road. I love their rawness and honesty in sharing their personal stories and also the way they've dealt with the practicalities and realities of RV living. I know it will inspire millions of people to live the life they've always dreamed of."

—Carolyn Tate, author of *The Purpose Project*

"We were beyond excited to hear *RVLove* was writing this book about the RV lifestyle, and we are honored to be a part of this incredible project and share our story with them. *RVLove* provides wonderful content, education, humor, and reality in all of their material, and we can't think of a better RV duo to write such a helpful piece of literature to share with the world through this book."

—Marissa and Nathan Moss of *Less Junk < More Journey*

"If you are thinking about or have already made the plunge into the mobile life with an RV, this book is for you. You're getting guidance from folks who have been actively RVing, with experiences and advice on what to watch out for and how to get the most enjoyment from your adventures. Use this book to enhance your experiences and fulfill your dreams of enjoying your RVing life. Above all, be safe out there!"

—Bruce Hopkins, VP of standards, RV Industry Association

LIVING the RV LIFE

YOUR ULTIMATE GUIDE TO LIFE ON THE ROAD

MARC and JULIE BENNETT of *RVLOVE*

ADAMS MEDIA

NEW YORK   LONDON   TORONTO   SYDNEY   NEW DELHI

▲ **adams**media

Adams Media
An Imprint of Simon & Schuster, Inc.
57 Littlefield Street
Avon, Massachusetts 02322

First Adams Media trade paperback edition November 2018

ADAMS MEDIA and colophon are trademarks of Simon & Schuster.

For information about special discounts for bulk purchases, please contact Simon & Schuster Special Sales at 1-866-506-1949 or business@simonandschuster.com.

The Simon & Schuster Speakers Bureau can bring authors to your live event. For more information or to book an event contact the Simon & Schuster Speakers Bureau at 1-866-248-3049 or visit our website at www.simonspeakers.com.

Interior design by Erin Alexander
Image credits listed at the end of this book

Manufactured in China

10 9 8 7 6 5 4 3 2 1

Library of Congress Cataloging-in-Publication Data has been applied for.

ISBN 978-1-5072-0898-4
ISBN 978-1-5072-0899-1 (ebook)

DEDICATION

To all those who lead "normal" lives, in the
hope you may be brave enough to choose
a new road that leads to more freedom and fun…
and embrace the inevitable twists and turns
as part of the adventure.

ACKNOWLEDGMENTS

This book was born from a series of serendipitous and fortuitous encounters that somehow all came together at exactly the right time and place, to end up in your hands at this moment. It all started over a chance meeting with an anonymous Floridian couple in a pizza restaurant in Colorado in July 2011. If that happens to be you reading this, just know that this whole crazy idea of us going full-time in an RV is all your fault. So, thanks! :)

In appreciation of the many full-time RVers who traveled the roads before us, shared your experiences, and (even if you don't know it) helped us along the way. To our incredible *RVLove* community who have followed our journey, supported us and inspired us to keep creating and sharing...we love you all! A huge shout-out to the entire RVing community and the many incredible people we've met on the road. There are too many to list here, but we remain grateful for our encounters, our time together (no matter how fleeting), your generosity, and your friendship.

A huge and heartfelt thank you to all of the RVers whose stories appear in this book—your honesty, experience, and insight helped bring each chapter to life: Jerome and Jennifer Braga (and Leighton and Shayla), Lisa and Dan Brown, Dawn and Mike Gondeck, Erik and Kala McCauley, Jennifer Meyer and Kate Hill, Caitlin and Tom Morton, Nathan and Marissa Moss (and Hensley), Becky and Tom Olesh, Stephen and Tanya Riley (and Donovan, Mason, and Emma), Peter and John of the RVgeeks, Joanne Shortell, Robert and Veronica Vaughan, Cherie Ve Ard and Chris Dunphy, Dee and Michael White, Nik and Allison White, and Freida Wolden. Thank you also to Eric Odom, the cast and crew of the *RV Nomads* movie, the team at ENTV, and many more who contributed stories and photographs to the creation of this book—we wish we could have included you all!

To our dear RVing friends Dennis & Donna Baril, thanks for your support, wisdom, insight, honesty, humor, and "peer-ental" guidance. Your love and friendship is truly a blessing.

High fives to our RV industry connections for continuing to impart your knowledge and experience with us, and our publishing team at Simon & Schuster/Adams Media—in particular Cate Coulacos Prato for seeking us out and guiding us throughout the publishing process, and Laura Daly for your editing wizardry! It truly takes a village...

Finally, *yay to you* for picking up the book and reading this—most people skip right past the Acknowledgments. We hope you love the book, and that it gets you on your way...no matter where you want to go, or how you choose to get there!

CONTENTS

Preface 9

Introduction 11

PART 1: GETTING STARTED / 13

CHAPTER 1: LIFE ON THE OPEN ROAD

What's It All About? **15**

What Is Full-Time RVing? 16

Why Are People Choosing the Full-Time RV Life? . . . 16

A Growing Movement 19

Who's Living the Full-Time RV Life? 20

RV Living versus Regular Home Living 22

Busting Common Myths and Misconceptions about the RV Lifestyle . . . 24

Quiz: Is the RV Life Right for You? 30

CHAPTER 2: SETTING YOURSELF UP FOR SUCCESS

Research, Prep, and Planning **31**

How Much Do RVs Cost? 32

What Does It Cost to Live in an RV? 36

To Sell or Not to Sell (Your House) 38

Create a Budget 42

Designing Your RV Lifestyle 44

When Can You Hit the Road? 48

Lightening Your Load: What to Do with All Your Stuff . . . 50

Next Steps 58

CHAPTER 3: FINDING YOUR HOME ON WHEELS

Choosing the Right RV Setup for You **59**

What Are the Different Types of RVs? 60

Where to Start Looking for RVs 68

The Most Important Considerations in Buying an RV:

Floor Plan and Quality Construction 70

Buying Your RV 73

How Does It Work?: Understanding Your RV 80

Staying Safe with Your RV 84

Dealing with RV Maintenance, Repairs, and Breakdowns . . . 90

PART 2: EMOTIONAL CONSIDERATIONS / 93

CHAPTER 4: TRANSITIONING TO RV LIFE

The Emotional Side of a Life Change **95**

Don't Underestimate the Emotional Transition 96

The Emotional Impact of Leaving Important Things: Your Home, Your Family, and Your Surroundings . . . 97

Living Together in a Small Space (Without Killing Each Other) . . . 100

Traveling with Kids 103

Traveling with Pets 106

Align On Your Travel Style and Pace Ahead of Time . . . 107

Managing the Logistics of RV Living 108

Making Your RV Feel Like Home 111

CHAPTER 5: STAYING CONNECTED

Keeping In Touch with People On and Off the Road . . **119**

Staying In Touch with Family and Friends Back Home 120

Finding Your Tribe on the Road 127

Building Your RV Community—Online and on the Road 130

Striking Up Conversations with Other RVers 139

Volunteering As an RVer 140

CHAPTER 6: LIVING FIT AND HEALTHY ON THE ROAD

Being Your Best Self **143**

Medical and Health Insurance 144

What Happens If You Get Sick? 149

Taking a Proactive Approach to Your Health 150

Creating Healthy Routines and Habits 156

What about Personal Safety? 164

PART 3: PRACTICAL CONSIDERATIONS / 169

CHAPTER 7: WORKING FROM THE ROAD

Earning Income While You Roam **171**

How Will You Be Working from the Road? 172

Other Ways to Make Money While Traveling 178

Should You Start a Blog or *YouTube* Channel? 182

Internet Solutions 186

Balancing Work, Life, and Travel 194

CHAPTER 8: LEGALLY SPEAKING

Domicile, Mail, Voting, Banking, and Taxes **197**

Choosing Your State of Domicile 198

How Do You Get Your Mail? 210

Banking and Credit Cards 216

Paying Taxes 219

CHAPTER 9: TRAVEL DESTINATIONS AND TRIP PLANNING

Let the Adventures Begin **221**

Where Do You Want to Go? 222

Planning a Route 223

When Should You Go? 226

Tips for Getting Good Driving Directions 228

Where to Stay 232

Save Money with RV and Camping Memberships 238

Crossing the Border: RVing to Canada and Mexico 241

Other Travel Options: Cheap Flights, Cruises, Traveling on Points, and Volunteerism 244

Off and Driving 248

Conclusion 250

Index 252

PREFACE

G'day! We're Marc and Julie Bennett. We're a married couple in our forties who lived a regular life in Colorado until June of 2014, when we sold our home, bought an RV, and hit the road to live, work, and travel full-time. Since then we have visited all fifty US states, plus Canada, Mexico, and Australia, and have no plans to stop anytime soon.

We found a way to unplug from society's definition of "success" and created our own, redesigning our lives around what we wanted—more freedom, love, and travel. We started a blog and a *YouTube* channel called *RVLove* and began sharing our journey.

Since hitting the road we've driven more than 40,000 miles in our RV, seen incredible places, and met more amazing people than we ever imagined. We've summered in Maine, wintered in the Arizona desert, hiked Colorado's Rocky Mountains, parasailed in the Florida Keys, cruised around Alaska, driven into Canada, and walked across the border into Mexico. We even spent a month in Australia, working at night and playing by day, swimming at beaches, exploring tropical rainforests, and snorkeling the Great Barrier Reef.

That's a lot of travel in a short time, and we've managed to do all this while still working full-time. No, we're not retired or wealthy! When we met in 2010, we were both starting over, rebuilding ourselves after life had knocked us down. Julie, an Australian, packed two suitcases and moved to America solo after her life and business imploded during the global financial crisis. A Colorado native, Marc was divorced and looking for a more compatible partner to share life's adventures with. We met on *eHarmony*, married in 2011, and started building a new future together in a modest townhome in the suburbs of Denver. We worked regular jobs, had two cars, took weekend road trips, and enjoyed annual vacations. Life was good, but daily stresses, big-city traffic, and Marc's health challenges slowly took their toll.

Like most Americans, Marc didn't get much vacation time from his job, and the effects of stress showed up in the form of physical, nerve-related illnesses. Something had to change, so we decided to start our lives over again…on the road! Now, we've been living in an RV longer than we lived in a regular home.

Through our RV life we found a way to lower stress, increase connection, and experience more adventure and travel, all while earning a living and saving for retirement. We reprioritized our goals, downsized our stuff, and took a leap of faith that changed our lives. It is absolutely doable, and we believe just about anyone can do this, if they really want it.

When we think back to when we first started—how little we knew, the time we spent planning and learning, the ups and downs of the emotional journey—we remember how confusing and overwhelming it was. Back then there were limited resources available, which is why we've been so passionate about sharing our journey to make the road smoother for others. Our blog and *YouTube* channel grew to the point where Marc was able to quit his job so we could focus on *RVLove* full-time. Since then we've created a ton of resources to help others learn how to successfully launch into their own RV life, including our online courses at RV Success School. Now, we've written this book and are getting ready to appear in a movie called *RV Nomads* with some of our fellow RVers on Epic Nomad TV.

RVing has opened doors we never could have imagined. It's been a life-changing journey of epic proportions, and we hope this book inspires you to live your own RV adventures, starting now!

INTRODUCTION

If you've been searching for ways to bring more freedom, fun, and travel into your life, you've come to the right book! We believe RVing is a fantastic way to live that offers all this and more.

In this book we'll share what the RV life is all about, what it offers, and just about everything you need to know to get you on your way. Many people are interested in RVing, but they get discouraged by what they see as obstacles—financial considerations, family, career, etc. But what if you didn't have to wait until retirement to go on long trips? What if you could find a way to live (and travel) on just about any budget? What if you could live an adventurous life while still working and parenting? Our goal is to show you how to make your RVing dreams a reality so you can start living these adventures sooner rather than later!

Life on the road is not all sunshine and rainbows, epic hikes, and national parks. We still wash dishes, work, and pay taxes. But when you're doing these things while living a fulfilled, adventurous life, they seem a lot easier to manage. We'll give you a solid, honest overview of what to expect—the good, the bad, and the in-between—and share the stories of a wide range of people living the RV life to help you decide if it's right for you.

It's a big life change, with many personal, financial, emotional, and practical considerations that need to be addressed. And we're here to walk you through them. Each chapter will better prepare you for the road ahead and help you get from where you are to where you want to be.

As you make your way through this book, you're going to have a lot of questions, and we'll have plenty for you too! We recommend that you take notes as you go along and start creating an action plan to keep you on track.

And while there's a lot to learn before, during, and after you hit the road, you'll find that this book offers loads of practical information, guidance, and useful resources to help you navigate the journey. Because it *is* a journey, and one that will take you to places that you never even imagined—around the country, throughout the world, and within yourself.

Are you ready? Buckle up! You're in for one heck of a ride!

PART 1

GETTING STARTED

With the promise of more travel, exciting adventures, better weather, and the chance to meet interesting new people, it's not surprising that the full-time RV lifestyle is becoming so popular. In Part 1 we'll cover what the RV lifestyle is all about and help you decide if it's for you—whether part-time or full-time. Next, we'll cover how to set yourself up for success when it comes to prep and planning. Then we'll introduce you to the different kinds of RVs to choose from and help you understand what features are important to have. Let's start by taking a peek at what an RV lifestyle can look like.

CHAPTER 1

LIFE ON THE OPEN ROAD

What's It All About?

"On your journey through life, make sure your biography has at least one extraordinary chapter."

—Unknown

Unless you know people living as full-time RVers or you've already spent time reading, learning, or watching videos about them, you probably don't know much about full-time RVing—yet. Why do people decide to uproot their lives to move into a home on wheels? Do RVs really break down a lot? Let's find out the answers to these questions and more, and then take a fun quiz to see if the RV life might be a good fit for you.

WHAT IS FULL-TIME RVING?

Full-timing in an RV generally means you live full-time—and likely travel—in a recreational vehicle, usually without having a physical home base to return to. Some full-time RVers travel extensively, while others may travel less often, spending multiple months in one location or area. Many sell everything to hit the road and some still own a home that they may leave vacant, rent out, or leave with a housesitter or family member to take care of, and may eventually plan to return to.

On the other hand, part-time RVers split their time between living in a traditional home and an RV, usually to escape cold winters or summer heat, or simply to travel more—they are often called snowbirds or sunbirds. They live in their RV seasonally or for extended periods, not just for weekends or vacations.

More than a million people (including us) have made an RV their home (and often their *only* home). And whether it's a motorhome, fifth wheel, or travel trailer, living in an RV gives you the freedom and flexibility to move anywhere, anytime—to have new experiences, meet new people, and see much more of the country and the world than you would if you lived in a stationary "stick and brick" home.

Let's take a deeper look at what's behind people even considering this lifestyle, and why it's becoming so popular.

WHY ARE PEOPLE CHOOSING THE FULL-TIME RV LIFE?

Until fairly recently, living in an RV full-time was considered something some people did when they retired—and usually only for a handful of years before age or health slowed them down. People assumed younger folks who were still working only had an RV for family vacations and weekend getaways. But today those ideas are being turned on their heads as the movement changes minds and public perception.

THE AMERICAN DREAM, REIMAGINED

Every year, thousands of people are waking up to the fact that the American Dream might not fit their idea of a great life. Go to college, get a good job, get married and have a family, buy a home and two cars, save for retirement, and live the good life once you hit sixty-five—it works for some people, but not everyone. Not only does that send us

the message that you have to wait until retirement to travel and really enjoy your life, but the truth is, the so-called American Dream has more people working longer and harder and trading their valuable time, health, and lives for money and material goods. And all that hard work and stress aren't necessarily getting people any closer to what they seem to really want in life: happiness and freedom.

You, and only you, are responsible for your future and, indeed, your own happiness and freedom. And while that's an uncomfortable—even scary—thought for some people, it's also incredibly liberating to realize that you actually do have a choice in how you live your life.

You get to decide what security, success, health, and happiness mean to you. You get to design your life on your own terms. Unfortunately, you're not encouraged to do that by most people around you—your employers, peers, family, friends, and authorities—so it's up to you to start asking different questions and looking for different answers—that is, if you want to change the course of your life and head in a new direction that is more exciting and rewarding for you.

> "Normal is getting dressed in clothes that you buy for work, driving through traffic in a car that you are still paying for, in order to get to a job that you need so you can pay for the clothes, car, and the house that you leave empty all day in order to afford to live in it."
>
> —*Ellen Goodman, American journalist*

Perhaps the idea of a "normal life" is becoming less appealing, as has been the case for us and thousands of others. Every day more and more people are choosing to step out of the box, explore new ways to live, increase their independence, and find—or, more accurately, create—their freedom. It's liberating to give yourself permission to redefine your life, reinvent yourself, and create your own new measures for success and happiness based on what is most important to you.

ASKING YOURSELF TOUGH QUESTIONS

If you feel unsettled and are longing for an adventurous RV life, take an active approach and ask yourself some big, important questions about what makes you happy. Is that big house, new car, latest iPhone, or 70-inch TV really your ultimate goal in life? Are those things actually making you happy?

What about your finances? Of course, paying for all of these toys and gadgets on credit can be way too easy! Accumulating more material stuff, thinking that it will make you happy, can almost be addictive. The problem is that the debt that can go along with these "upgrades" to your life causes a great deal of stress—and a feeling of entrapment that is hard to escape. You have to work to pay for the things you bought.

The truth is, many people are locked into this type of system, and often, everyone else around them has bought into it as well. Perhaps you were brought up this way, too, and you didn't know any different. There's no one to blame. It's just the way things are, and it's been that way for many years.

"So many people say 'you're living my dream,' but most don't do anything about living their own. If more people spent even just a little time looking into it, they would realize this dream is a lot more achievable than they ever imagined."

—*Julie Bennett, coauthor of this book*

But eventually you may reach your own tipping point and start asking yourself some honest questions, with an inner dialogue that goes something like this:

What am I doing? My life isn't working for me anymore. I'm not happy. It seems like I'm constantly busy, stressed, getting sick, overwhelmed, and feeling unfulfilled…and so is everyone else around me. Is this all there is to life? When do I get to LIVE? Do I really have to wait until I'm sixty-five!? Aaarrrggghhh!

These feelings of confusion, unhappiness, and unrest can make your life pretty uncomfortable. Why not get honest with yourself, challenge "the norm" and the way we've all been taught is "the right way to live," and start to consider your alternatives?

A GROWING MOVEMENT

More than a million people in North America have already found a better way to live that works for them. According to the Recreation Vehicle Industry Association (RVIA), as of 2018 almost 10 million US households own an RV, but these are mostly used for recreational purposes—on weekends and during the precious little vacation time most Americans get from their jobs—on average just a couple of weeks a year. While this type of recreational and vacation RVing isn't anything new, the idea of living full-time in an RV has been around for decades but has become increasingly popular in recent years. There is no formal organization or entity that tracks (or is likely even able to track) the true number of full-time RVers—because the number changes daily, many are constantly on the move, and some even live off the grid—so the number is impossible to report with any accuracy. However, it is equally impossible to ignore the trends that are fueling the growth of the full-time RVing movement: advancements in cellular technology enabling remote work and affordable, accessible connectivity; record RV shipments for the eighth consecutive year (according to the RVIA, more than 500,000 units were shipped in 2017); and rapidly growing social media interest groups about full-time RVing.

A large and fast-growing community—roughly estimated at between 1.3 and 1.8 million people—choose to live, travel, and often work from their RV full-time as their primary residence. And millions more do it part-time or seasonally—for three to six months at a time—to escape the cold winters, usually from the northern US and Canada.

Solo travelers, couples, and families alike—of all ages—are hitting the road in droves. This more nomadic type of lifestyle can be difficult for many people to understand because it's so…not normal! Who are these people really? Let's find out.

WHO'S LIVING THE FULL-TIME RV LIFE?

It can be easy to make assumptions about the kinds of people who would choose to live in an RV, whether it's a motorhome or truck and trailer—but these stereotypes are largely inaccurate. Sure, some RVers are retired—but some work remotely, while others are creating new businesses from the road. Some do "work camping" or have young families. RVers come from all financial backgrounds—some stay in upscale RV parks, others camp in more modest campgrounds, and some spend their time "boondocking"—also known as dry camping—off the grid without being connected to utilities. Some may park their RV in one place to use as a permanent residence, while others use it to travel and explore the country or even the world.

They may be of different ages and life stages, come from different walks of life, have differing financial means, and have different reasons for doing it, but they can be found living all around North America—and the world.

Here are some examples of the kinds of people you might meet over the years—people who willingly chose to "give it all up" for life on the road in an RV:

- **Millennials** looking for ways to travel and explore various career options on their quest for more meaning and adventure (while staying digitally connected).

- **Baby boomers** seeking an affordable, exciting way to enjoy their retirement, take their pets along, be of service by volunteering, and visit family while seeing the country.

- **Pre-retirees** looking for ways to start easing into retirement by transitioning their careers to working remotely, perhaps with part-time hours or by consulting for their employers.

- **Gen Xers** wanting to take their jobs on the road to work remotely or start a business that supports their desire for more balance, freedom, and travel, while saving for retirement (that's us!).

- **Burned-out career professionals** trying to reduce their stress and reclaim their health and life by taking an extended road trip to hit the reset button.

- **Families** aiming to reconnect and spend more time together, share adventures, and create memories, often while homeschooling their kids so they can learn via real-world, hands-on experiences.

- **People considering relocation** and wanting to travel around the country while they explore and research new places to set down roots.

- **Those wanting to simplify their life,** reduce debt, and save for their financial future and goals.

- **Those wanting to embrace minimalism,** live frugally, and increase their independence and self-sufficiency while living off the grid.

What do they all have in common?

1. They all have a desire to unplug from society's "normal" way of life and take more control over their lives, creating their own definition of happiness and success.

2. They all want to experience more travel and freedom.

3. They are open to achieving these goals through an RV lifestyle.

RV LIVING VERSUS REGULAR HOME LIVING

As you consider RV living, it can be helpful to know what won't change as well as what will. Let's talk about some of the similarities and differences between RV living and living in a regular home.

WHAT'S SIMILAR?

There are more similarities between living in an RV and living in a regular home than you might expect.

- **RVs have basic necessities:** Many standard aspects of a regular home are also in a home on wheels: four walls, a roof, and a floor, to start! Most RVs—certainly the ones you would probably want to live in—come with a kitchen counter and sink, refrigerator, stovetop, microwave and/or convection oven, and sometimes even a regular oven. You'll also have a toilet and shower, bed, closet, storage cupboards, sofa, dining table, seating, and anywhere from one to four TVs!

- **RVs can be very luxurious:** Many "upgrades" are also available in RVs, such as a washer/dryer, dishwasher, residential fridge/freezer with ice maker and water purifier, entertainment system, bathtub, in-floor heating, and much more.

You can easily connect to electricity, water, and sewer when hooked up at an RV park or campground, so the RVs that many people choose to live in are actually very comfortable, and a lot of us aren't roughing it as much as you might think! You can have all of your basic needs met, and often much more, when living in an RV.

Tom, 32, and Cait, 28

FULL-TIME RVERS SINCE SEPTEMBER 2015

Website: www.mortonsonthemove.com
YouTube: Mortons on the Move
Instagram: @mortonsonthemove
Facebook: Mortons on the Move

> "The RV lifestyle enables us to do the things we want, in the places we want to be, with the people we want to be with."

AFTER GRADUATING FROM COLLEGE, GETTING GOOD-PAYING corporate jobs (Cait in business IT, Tom in electrical engineering), getting married, and buying a house, we found the "American Dream" wasn't working for us. We felt stuck in a programmed life—in our house, our jobs, our daily commute, and Michigan's long, gray winters. We wanted to move but didn't know where, as we barely had enough vacation time to visit family for the holidays, let alone explore. We wanted to change our jobs but didn't know what we wanted to do, and the dream of starting our own businesses seemed untouchable. Our five-year plan was mapped out, unexciting, and seemed like someone else's life.

The idea of full-time RV life came to us on our way back from a trip to Florida, while driving two hours home from the airport in a typical Michigan blizzard, wishing there was a way for us to work remotely from wherever we wanted. We drove by an RV dealership and Tom said, "Don't people live in those?" By the time we got home, we'd decided we were going to sell everything and move into an RV! It seemed to solve all of our problems so we could explore the country, avoid winter, follow the sun, focus on our health, and find rewarding work by starting our own businesses.

While the idea of selling everything and finding freedom on the open road was exhilarating, we also wanted to be responsible. We did extensive research and budgeting to figure out how long we could travel without hurting our financial future. Fortunately, besides our mortgage we were debt-free. We bought a used RV and truck to avoid having any debt or monthly payments once we hit the road. We determined we could RV for about two years without making any money so we could redesign our lives: start our own businesses, see the country, and have the adventure of a lifetime!

It took a year and a half to get ready. We sold our house, cars, most of our furniture and possessions, two horses, and we even sent our cat to live with Cait's parents. We hit the road with our two dogs, Mocha and Bella, and became "Mortons on the Move."

Today we are thriving in the RV lifestyle with no end in sight! We've found multiple streams of income—from odd jobs off *Craigslist* to remote contract positions. We started several businesses that enable us to work remotely, including a blog and *YouTube* channel to document our adventures and educate others, an e-commerce store, and a digital media company.

Our RV life has opened doors we'd never dreamed about, introduced us to many dear friends we would never have met, and allowed us to see more places and have more adventures than we ever could have had in our previous life. Our new five-year plan is full of adventures and unknowns—and that sounds perfect to us!

WHAT'S DIFFERENT?

Clearly, some things aren't the same. For example:

- **RVs are smaller:** One of the biggest differences between an RV and a regular home is the size. RVs are almost always much smaller than regular homes (the exceptions being very small apartments and tiny homes). However, the design, layout, and storage are usually much more efficient in an RV, to make the best use of the space.

- **RVs can move:** Of course, one of the best things about living in an RV is that you can move it! Travel becomes part of your everyday life, and you have the ability to change location whenever you choose, to optimize weather conditions or visit a new place.

- **RVs help you reconnect with nature:** An RV gives you the ability to live off the grid for days or weeks at a time, which can be very liberating, as it allows you to stay out in nature with all the comforts of home—but without being plugged into utilities.

There are many misconceptions and incorrect assumptions about RVing floating around. Let's put some of those into perspective.

BUSTING COMMON MYTHS AND MISCONCEPTIONS ABOUT THE RV LIFESTYLE

MYTH #1: RVS ARE EXPENSIVE

Though it is true that some luxury RVs cost well over a million dollars, they are the rare exception, not the rule. We have met people who happily live full-time in RVs that cost under $10,000, and many who have spent $200,000 or more. However, the majority of full-time RVers we meet seem to have spent somewhere between $50,000 and $150,000 on their RV setup (including tow vehicle). And since most RVs have kitchens, bathrooms, and sleeping areas, you can often get a long-term loan with a monthly payment, just like a home mortgage. The type of RV you buy and how you choose to travel may vary, but you can RV on virtually any budget.

MYTH #2: RVS GET TERRIBLE MILEAGE AND COST A FORTUNE IN FUEL

While it is true that some RVs (in particular, larger motorhomes) get poor mileage compared to most passenger vehicles, it's important to remember that you will probably not drive an RV like a passenger vehicle. You may drive your RV a few hundred miles and then stay in one location for days, weeks, or months at a time.

In addition, many full-time RVers tow a separate vehicle to use for errands and exploring, which will get better mileage and help average out fuel costs. It's entirely possible to spend less on fuel traveling the country than you do now, living locally.

MYTH #3: RVS ARE TOO SMALL TO LIVE IN COMFORTABLY

Actually, some RVs are larger than small apartments, but even small RVs usually have well-designed, comfortable spaces that can provide everything you need. That, plus the fact that you are usually in locations with great weather and changing scenery, tends to make your space feel large, not confining. You may sleep and work inside your RV, but you tend to spend more time outdoors so you live in a much larger space that encompasses every area you travel to. By contrast, many people have never lived outside of their state, their city, or even the small town where they were born. If you ask us, that is living in a small space.

MYTH #4: RVS ARE ALWAYS BREAKING AND IN THE SHOP

Bad news travels faster than good news, and complainers love to be heard. So when somebody talks about how their RV keeps breaking or spends significant time in the repair shop, people will usually spread the story. Sure, things on RVs do break and need fixing, but it's often only little things and many you can fix yourself if you're handy. If you buy a decent-quality RV and take good care of it with regular maintenance, you can minimize many issues. Repairs and breakdowns are not uncommon, but can also be relative to usage.

Perhaps we've been lucky, but in the four-plus years (more than 1,500 days) we have been living in our RV full-time, we have needed to stay out of our RV for repairs for only about ten days, AND in almost every case we got to plan ahead and choose the days. That is a pretty small percentage of time, around 1 percent. And while some RVs might end up in the shop more than others, we believe most RVs spend the vast majority of the time being enjoyed.

RVs are certainly not perfect, you *will* experience issues (just as you would in a home), and the frustration or stress of RV repairs will be amplified if you are new to RVing, or in an unfamiliar area.

MYTH #5: THE RV LIFE IS LONELY

While it can take time to build a community of friends on the road, we have found that many RVers, especially full-timers, are very open, friendly people. At the same time, you can choose to be as social or private as you wish. Technology makes it easy for you to stay in touch with people, and there are RVing groups you can join to meet others. And because people tend to spend more time outside; are less caught up in the stress and busyness of chores and other aspects of "regular" life; and often have more flexible schedules, there are more opportunities to be social and make new friends. You might find, as we did, that your RV life is much more socially active than your regular life was.

MYTH #6: PEOPLE WHO LIVE IN RVS ARE BROKE AND LIVE IN TRAILER PARKS

The many different types of people living in RVs may surprise you. While it is true that many people live in RVs, trailers, or trailer parks because it is more affordable than living in a traditional home or neighborhood, there are also plenty of folks who choose the RV life so they can travel in comfortable, modern, and even luxurious trailers and motorhomes—that can be just as nice or even nicer than many houses and condos—and stay in upscale RV parks.

MYTH #7: YOU CAN'T RV UNLESS YOU ARE RETIRED OR WEALTHY

The flip side of the previous myth is that you have to be rich and retired to begin full-time RVing. While we do meet a lot of financially comfortable people on the road, we have also met thousands who aren't but have found a way to make the RV life work for them, regardless of their situation or financial means. Whether people sold their house to buy an RV, saved diligently, took their jobs on the road, or just found a way to be extremely resourceful with their limited funds, we never cease to be amazed and inspired by the many and varied ways that people make their RV dream a reality. You will find people who live on $700 a month and others who spend more than $7,000 a month, but most fall somewhere in between $2,500 and $3,500 per month. You can almost always find a way to make RVing work for you, no matter how much or how little money you may have.

MYTH #8: YOU CAN'T RV FULL-TIME WITH KIDS

Lots of families RV full-time with children of all ages—from newborns to late teens. Parents traveling with their families are common, perhaps even more common than similar-aged travelers who don't have children. We've seen families with one child all the way up to large families with twelve kids living in an RV! There's a large, active community of full-time RVing families who help and support one another on the road. Some families RV for a year, while others do it long term, but there's definitely a big and thriving full-time family community on the road, and ways to educate kids along the way (more on that in Chapter 4).

> ## RV TERMS TO KNOW
>
> **roadschooling:** Homeschooling children from the road; educating through the experience of visiting landmarks and attractions.

MYTH #9: BUYING AN RV IS A TERRIBLE FINANCIAL DECISION

It can be, but it doesn't have to be. Although it is true that an RV is an asset that will (almost always) depreciate in value over time (just like a car), you might find the depreciation to be comparable to the hidden costs of home ownership or renting. While real estate generally tends to appreciate over time, the costs of property taxes, utility bills, homeowners' association (HOA) fees, trash service, and maintenance are often overlooked when it comes to the total cost of owning a home. As an RVer, you rarely pay any of those costs (except for RV repairs and maintenance), and you save on the cost of furniture, which is almost always included in the RV. For renters paying "dead money" to a landlord, an RV can provide an alternative way to live while also saving money—as long as you shop and spend wisely.

MYTH #10: AS AN RVER, YOU LIVE A STORYBOOK, WORRY-FREE LIFE

The realities of RV life are not just what you see in an *Instagram* feed. Sure, you get to travel and explore more often than most, but that isn't what every day looks like. RV life comes with its own challenges—juggling work, making RV repairs, and doing chores are all part of the lifestyle—but these are things you'd be doing in your "regular" life anyway! And if you reduce financial stress and job unhappiness, the challenges won't seem as bad anymore. Manage your expectations, realize you'll have ups and downs, and remember that your attitude will play a big part in your experience.

Welcome!
Registration is Easy!

① FIND AN EMPTY CAMPSITE

② NOTE THE SITE NUMBER &
YOUR LICENSE PLATE NUMBER

③ RETURN TO THE CLOSEST
PAY STATION

④ FOLLOW PROMPTS &
TAKE RECEIPT

ENJOY YOUR STAY!

www.cityofseward.us

FEE AREA

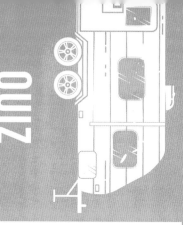

QUIZ

Is the RV Life Right for You?

It's up to you, and only you, to decide if RVing is something you want to explore further. Take a few minutes to answer the following questions to get an idea of whether or not the RV lifestyle might be a good fit for you. Have your traveling companion(s) do the exercise, too, and compare your answers.

If you answered "Yes" to at least half of these questions, then the full-time RV lifestyle could be a fit for you. And if you answered "Yes" to most of these questions, you will likely love it!

1. Are you interested in traveling more?

2. Do you like seeing new places and experiencing new things?

3. Do you consider yourself to be adventurous or courageous?

4. Are you reasonably happy with your life but still have a longing for something more?

5. Would you like to visit people or places in other parts of the country?

6. Have you ever wished you could bring your pets along on more vacations or trips?

7. Do you want to make the most of your health and wellness while you have them?

8. Are you able to earn money remotely, or are you willing to explore new ways to do so?

9. Do you enjoy driving and road trips?

10. Do you get tired of hot summers or cold winters and want to spend more time in optimal weather?

11. Do you ever feel like having so much "stuff" in your house weighs you down?

12. Do you ever get tired of yard work or shoveling snow?

13. Do you like meeting new people?

14. Are you willing to be flexible when things don't go according to plan?

15. Do you have a good sense of humor?

16. Do you know—or are you willing to learn—how to use basic tools for simple repairs?

17. Do you ever feel stressed out, craving a simpler, less complicated life?

18. Would you like to spend more time in nature?

19. Would you like to have more control over your expenses and budget?

20. Do you like the idea of becoming more self-sufficient and confident?

21. Do you want to spend more time with your loved ones and create more memories together?

22. Do you want to create a lifestyle that is more aligned with your desires and goals?

23. Are you limited financially and looking for ways to live a more comfortable, adventurous life?

CHAPTER 2

SETTING YOURSELF UP FOR SUCCESS

Research, Prep, and Planning

"Planning is bringing the future into the present so that you can do something about it now."

—Alan Lakein, American author

Before you start shopping for your RV, there's a lot to research and consider about how your life will change. Things like budgeting, downsizing, and possibly even selling your home are all big and important decisions, and the level of complexity or simplicity will be different for everyone. If you're a twenty-something with no kids and few responsibilities, it may be easier and more fun for you to jump in and learn as you go, as that could be part of the adventure. But if you own a home, are approaching retirement, have an established career and/or have kids in school, there's a lot more at stake. There's no need to rush into this! You want to be certain that RVing is right for you, and with the proper preparation you can move forward with confidence and avoid many common mistakes. In this chapter you'll gain a solid understanding of what to expect when planning for your RV life, so you can make sound decisions that you feel really good about and design an RV lifestyle that works for you.

HOW MUCH DO RVS COST?

RVs range in cost from around $2,000 (used) to well over $2 million (new), but the majority of people we meet who live full-time in their RVs spent between $50,000 and $150,000.

The cost of your RV is not necessarily related to how much you enjoy the experience. The interesting thing is that almost every RVer we have met—regardless of what they spent on their RV or pay in monthly expenses—loves the RV lifestyle and what it offers them. Their happiness is more about the freedom to travel and live as they choose than about how expensive or fancy their RV is. We all get to enjoy the same sunsets, national parks, and beaches, regardless of what we drive and live in! But we all have our own personal tastes and standards of living, too, and every RVer wants to find an RV that feels like home. Keep in mind that you can buy a very nice, good-quality used RV for far less than a brand-new, lower-quality RV, and you should never spend more than what's financially comfortable for you.

FINANCING THE PURCHASE

Buying an RV is generally easy, as banks will often offer fifteen- and even twenty-year loans on RVs, keeping your payments affordable. There are some caveats to that, which we'll speak more about in the next chapter.

It's also important to keep in mind that RVs, unlike most homes, will depreciate over time. Depreciation is a hidden cost of RV ownership that many fail to take into consideration when budgeting for their RV life. This will vary widely depending on the age and cost of the RV you buy, but to give you an example, we bought our first RV when it was two years old for just under $100,000, including tax. Our payment was about $570 per month on a twenty-year loan. When we sold it four years later for $75,000 and factored in the depreciation loss over that time, it averaged out at $520 per month, so in real financial terms, our RV cost us closer to $1,100 per month. As a very rough guide for now, you might consider doubling your RV payment when factoring depreciation into your budget, but know that it can be much higher or lower, depending on what you buy. Think of it like buying a car and not a house, as almost anything with wheels will depreciate. The moral of the story is: don't underestimate the effects of depreciation!

TRAVEL AND CAMPGROUND EXPENSES

Once you have purchased your RV, the next biggest expense depends on your travel style and where you stay. You may choose to make the most of the fact that your RV is equipped with the ability to provide water and electricity in the middle of free, public lands (commonly called BLM land—Bureau of Land Management land), and therefore you may not stay in RV parks or campgrounds very often. Or you may prefer the comforts of a campsite with water, electricity, and other amenities offered in an RV park, like a swimming pool, hot tub, laundry, lodge, and sporting courts, or even a high-end resort with manicured grounds, a gym, and paved, level sites. It's also possible to stay very affordably in RV parks and campgrounds that offer a camping membership (that's what we often do), which can lower your camping costs substantially. We'll talk more about these options in Chapter 9.

RV resort fees in popular places at peak times can be as high as $200 or more a night, and yes, that is with you supplying your own RV! But that is the exception, not the rule. In general, RV parks and campgrounds tend to average around $30–$50/night. These fees can be much cheaper in some areas, especially when staying for a month or more at a time, but the lowest nightly rate we've seen is about $10–$15.

At this point you might be thinking that staying outside of campgrounds is looking very financially appealing. But keep in mind that when camping "off-grid" you'll still need to find a place to refill your water and dump wastewater, which often comes with a fee, and of course, you'll eventually need to do your laundry too. Equipping your RV with electricity for camping off-grid usually involves fuel costs to run a generator, upgrading your battery bank or installing solar panels, which can be a worthwhile investment if you are planning on doing a lot of dry camping.

To give you a ballpark estimate of what to expect, in our first four years of full-time RVing we spent about 80 percent of our time in RV parks and campgrounds, and averaged between $400 and $600 per month in campground fees. We spent about 20 percent of our time boondocking or dry camping off-grid on free public lands, overnighting in a Walmart parking lot during a cross-country drive, or staying on a friend's property. Some months we might not spend anything (due to our camping membership), and other months we might splurge and spend $1,000 on a much nicer RV park, so we tend to look at our annualized campground expenditure and then come up with a monthly average. Again, we know RVers who mostly boondock and spend less than $100 per month on camping fees, and others who consistently spend over $1,000 or even $2,000 per month on campsite-related fees (hello, winter in the Florida Keys!). We recently upgraded our RV by installing new lithium batteries and solar panels to enable us to spend more time off the grid and in nature, so we expect our future monthly camping fees will be much lower as a result.

Remember, these costs are all variable depending on how, when, and where you like to travel. Think about the kinds of places you might like to stay if you plan to camp off-grid, and what you're willing or able to spend on monthly camping fees.

FUEL COSTS

Your next expense is fuel for driving your RV and vehicle (if you have one), and while this can be high for some, it may surprise you to learn that we actually spend less on fuel now than many we know who live a more traditional life with two cars commuting daily to work. Yes, it's true that motorhomes and large trucks towing trailers generally won't get great fuel economy, but remember, if you are moving less frequently, you may not be traveling that many miles and therefore won't need much fuel. Some move their RVs only once a month, or maybe only twice a year for snowbirds and seasonal workers, while other RVers prefer a faster-paced travel style. Perhaps you're on a mission to see as much of the country as possible in a year and will be on the move every few days. Because we still work, ideally we try to situate ourselves for two- to three-week stays and even as long as a month at a time, so we can work and explore the local area at a more relaxed pace. Just keep in mind that you are the one who gets to decide how far and how often you travel, so you can control your fuel cost to keep it in line with your budget.

Consider that when your RV is your home, you are typically traveling in one direction, while vacationers will head to a destination and then must go back, which of course doubles the miles. For example, in 2015 we started the year in

San Diego, California, made our way through the central US and up to Maine for the summer, then traveled down the East Coast, and finished up the year in Miami, Florida, visiting a total of thirty-three states in the process. That year we put just 8,408 miles on the RV and 11,407 on our towed vehicle (a Mini Cooper Convertible)—that's a total of 19,815 miles in a year of living and traveling to more than half the country! According to the US Department of Transportation, the average driver puts more than 13,000 miles a year on their car which adds up to almost 27,000 miles for a household with two cars. Our big advantage is that we work from home (our RV) and don't have a daily commute. Our tow vehicle gets much better gas mileage than our RV, and that is what we use for errands and exploring. So our total annual miles are much lower than the average and yet we get to travel and explore the country!

Some months we spend more on fuel and some months we spend less, but in four years of full-time RV travel, our fuel costs have always averaged between $300 and $400 per month. Of course, we also know RVers who spend way more and others who spend way less. Try saving your fuel receipts to determine how much you spend each month on fuel for all your vehicles and see what it adds up to. That will be a good starting point for your budget.

OTHER EXPENSES

Other expenses related to your RV lifestyle include insurance, vehicle registration, upgrades, repairs, and maintenance. These may be comparable to the cost of insurance, repairs, and maintenance for your home and second vehicle, so add up those costs to estimate what these expenses may be like for your RV. Again, these costs can vary widely depending on your situation and chosen RV and vehicles, but it's a good starting point.

Your general living expenses will remain fairly consistent, regardless of whether you are living in an RV or a traditional home. As you further your research and refine your travel goals, you'll find additional resources to help you save money on your travels (we cover some of those in Chapter 9).

WHAT DOES IT COST TO LIVE IN AN RV?

This is one of the most common questions we get. It can be difficult to assess whether or not you can afford the RV lifestyle without having any idea of the related expenses. The good news is that we know people in every income bracket and financial situation who have found a way to make the RV life work for them. The majority spends around $2,500–$3,500 per month (couples and families), if being conscious about spending.

It's difficult to specify the exact cost of RV living because it depends on such a wide range of variables and choices you make. In general, most RVers agree that your RV lifestyle will tend to cost pretty close to what you currently spend in your regular lifestyle.

The amount you'll spend really depends on your RVing goals. If the RV life is your retirement reward after decades of saving, and you buy your dream RV so you can winter at high-end RV resorts in the Florida Keys, your expenses will be higher than most. If you're on a fixed income and looking for ways to stretch your budget, you can buy an inexpensive RV and live a more frugal, yet still very enjoyable, life. If your goal is to reduce debt, make an early career change, or save for your financial future, your expenses will likely be significantly lower than in your traditional lifestyle.

The reason your RV lifestyle will cost close to the same as your current lifestyle is that most people like to maintain similar standards of living, regarding a comfortable home, amenities, eating out, and other spending habits. Of course, things like groceries and general living expenses will carry over to your life on wheels, regardless of how and where you live.

RV Expenses Overview

Here's an overview of the typical expenses you can expect in your RV lifestyle:

RV-SPECIFIC EXPENSES

- RV purchase (plus tax, loan payments, and interest)
- Insurance
- Extended service contract (optional)
- Repairs and maintenance
- Fuel for driving
- Propane for cooking, heating, and refrigerator
- RV parks and campgrounds

If you buy your RV as a second home, these expenses will be on top of what you already pay for your mortgage, rent, and related expenses. However, if you plan on selling your home to live full-time in your RV, many of your existing home-related expenses will go away and be replaced by these.

Your regular living expenses that will continue in your RV life might look something like this:

REGULAR LIVING EXPENSES

- Groceries
- Entertainment and eating out
- Internet/cell phones
- Health insurance
- Personal care (e.g., hair, dental)
- Pets (e.g., vet, food)
- Gifts (e.g., birthdays, holidays)
- Other luxuries, like treats and other travel/vacations

TO SELL OR NOT TO SELL (YOUR HOUSE)

Now that we have addressed the biggest expenses that you will encounter on the road, let's talk about what is perhaps the biggest factor in the affordability of the full-time RV lifestyle: what you plan to do with your traditional home. If you're a homeowner, trying to support your regular household and an RV at the same time can get expensive, but if you are able to trade one for the other, as we did, the finances get easier really quickly.

What Is Your Traditional Life Costing You?

You may still be wondering how you're going to afford all this, so let's take a look at where your money is going now to see how and where things add up. Here are the typical expenses incurred by many homeowners:

- Home mortgage
- Property taxes
- Utilities (water, electric, gas)
- Homeowners' association (HOA) fees

- Insurance
- Furnishings and décor
- Maintenance, repairs, and upgrades
- Landscaping and yard work
- Services, such as house cleaner
- Stuff (because you have the space, you just keep buying it!)

When you look at the fixed expenses related to home ownership—say, the first four items on this list—you'll quickly start to see how they add up and could be reallocated to the cost of your RV and campgrounds. You rarely need to buy furniture for an RV—unless you're renovating it—and utility bills are generally included in campground fees (except for monthly stays). With no more property taxes, homeowners' association fees, or yard work either, you may be starting to see the financial appeal of RVing—IF you properly plan and budget and buy your RV well! You probably won't need more than one car, so consider what you'll save there. And let's not forget all the "stuff" you can stop buying!

MAKING THE DECISION

Once you take stock of what you're currently spending, your decision might become clearer. Following are other factors to consider.

IF YOU CURRENTLY RENT

If you currently rent, the financial tradeoff is pretty straightforward. You simply trade the money you normally spend on rent and utilities for an RV payment and camping fees.

IF YOU WANT TO SELL YOUR HOME

If you own (or have a mortgage on) a home, the decision becomes more complex and individualized. If you are looking for a fresh start or a new place to live, you'll likely want to sell your home, perhaps with the intention of buying somewhere else in the future. Selling your home will be the most freeing of all options since you won't need to manage and maintain a property, especially from afar. We found that releasing our permanent ties to the area gave us more mental and emotional freedom as well. Again, this is a very personal decision, and only you can decide what is right for you.

IF YOU WANT TO KEEP—BUT RENT OUT—YOUR HOME

If you are planning to take a "sabbatical" year to give yourself a break but generally love your home and community, then perhaps renting out your current home (or part of it) is a better option. If you aren't sure if you'll like the RV life and want to try it out for a while, you may not want to sell your home right away. In this case, moving out of your traditional home and renting it out can be a good way to subsidize your life on the road. There are rental management companies that can manage the property for you, and while they do charge a fee, they also take care of things so you can be free of most worries to enjoy your travels. Plus, as real estate typically (though not always) appreciates over time, keeping your home as a financial asset while also earning rental income helps offset the depreciation of your RV. Property owners are also viewed favorably by lenders, which may help you get a better interest rate while improving your chances of getting RV financing approved.

IF YOU WANT TO KEEP YOUR HOME (WITHOUT RENTING IT OUT)

If you are in the financial position to comfortably maintain both a traditional home and an RV, then you can test out the lifestyle more gradually by taking extended trips to see if you like RVing. This is a great option, especially if you have a partner or family who isn't fully committed to the idea of RVing. It can be comforting for some to maintain a home base, knowing they still have the security of their home to return to, especially if RVing doesn't work out. They may discover that they love RVing and feel ready to let go of the home later, but it may be too much to consider all at once. Or maybe you (or they) won't like it as much as you thought, and your travels will be short lived. This is something you'll need to discuss and work through together to find an agreeable plan.

CREATE A BUDGET

Planning for the financial aspects of an RV life involves looking at where you currently spend your money and how you can reallocate that toward funding a lifestyle that you may be more excited about. It may require a shift in perspective, some creativity, and a change in your spending habits, but it's absolutely doable. Using the information you've learned already in this chapter, create a spreadsheet that itemizes all of your expenses in your current life (monthly and annual), separating them into fixed and variable expenses.

One of the benefits of the RV lifestyle is the flexibility and variability of expenses, compared to traditional lifestyles that typically involve fixed payments for rent, HOA fees, utilities, car payments, average fuel costs for driving to work, and so on. Remember, most households have two cars and most RVers need only one car, as there's not usually a work commute. When you live in an RV, your fixed expenses are usually only an RV payment (if you finance), insurance, and regular maintenance. Expenses such as RV parks, campgrounds, and fuel are considered variable, as you have more control over them than you would in a traditional life. Let's say, for example, you were hit with an unexpected bill of $2,000. In your traditional life, you would still have to pay your regular fixed expenses, but in the RV life these are generally lower and you have more flexibility to slow down your travels and stay put for a while to save money on fuel and camping fees while you get caught up.

As an RVer, the variability of your expenses allows you to create an entirely new lifestyle in which you can choose to spend more or less than you do currently, but your current spending should still be the baseline it is measured against—that is, unless you have a specific goal to either save more money on the road OR kick up your heels and spend it all on your way out! Just remember that RVing is a lifestyle, not a vacation, so you'll need to resist the temptation to travel faster and spend more like you would on a short vacation.

GET RID OF DEBT

Pay off as much debt as possible before hitting the road. You may have an RV payment, like a home mortgage or rent, but try to avoid taking credit card or other unsecured debt with you on the road. Unless you already have the income to service those debts in your RV life, trying to find ways to make money while juggling debt will just create stress. Focus on paying off your debts first so you can hit the road with a clean slate and the fewest expenses possible. Less debt lightens your load and allows you to really enjoy the freedom that the RV life offers.

We have seen people hit the road with big visions of the lifestyle who started out burdened by debt, which reduced their financial sustainability, eventually forced them off the road, and even dug them into a deeper financial hole. Don't be one of them! Yes, you can live the RV lifestyle on the cheap, but if you bring along too much debt from your old life, it will just be stressful and challenging and defeat the whole purpose of living a life of freedom.

"Full-time RVing is exciting and rewarding, but it is still real life. Planning for retirement, having adequate funds for living expenses, and making a plan for emergencies are crucial. While RV life is nomadic and has a sense of freedom, there is still a need for personal responsibility to earn a living and be self-supporting."

—*Dawn Gondeck, full-time RVer*

If you plan to ease into RV living by keeping your home, you'll need to financially support both lifestyles simultaneously for a while, so factor that into your budgeting. Of course, if you do decide to go "all in" by fully transitioning from your regular life to the full-time RV life, you will likely end up trading your current lifestyle expenses for your RV lifestyle expenses. If you're careful with your spending and will be saying goodbye to hefty property taxes, you may even end up better off!

BE SURE TO ADD IN OTHER LIVING EXPENSES

While the typical variable expenses of your traditional lifestyle—like groceries, eating out, pets, health, and personal care—may be similar on the road, be prepared for some adjustment. You won't be buying groceries in bulk anymore, so it may seem like you're paying more, but you'll probably find that you waste less too. There's a good chance you may spend more on restaurants and eating out, as you'll always be somewhere new and may want to try the local cuisine or visit attractions, so keep an eye on that or plan to budget a bit more for eating out and entertainment. And depending on your healthcare situation, those costs may vary as well (we'll talk more about healthcare in Chapter 6). Just know that many of your current expenses will be traded for new ones.

Other things you might want to factor into your budgeting include return visits to your hometown to visit family, friends, or doctors. Depending on where you are in the country, it may not always make sense to return via RV, so budget in airfares or alternate forms of travel for those situations.

DESIGNING YOUR RV LIFESTYLE

Now let's look at how you can make living on the road work for YOU. One of the most exciting things about entertaining the idea of the RV lifestyle is that you get to consciously design your life the way you want it to be. If you've never done this before, you're not alone. This is a simple yet powerful exercise that will help you gain clarity and guide your planning and choices.

The first step in designing your life and setting yourself up for success is to establish your overall goal and vision for your RV life, travels, and experiences. We call it defining your "why." You may find that what you come up with is vastly different than how you're living now, and that's okay. You're not running away from your old life so much as moving closer to the one you want. Be intentional about it to ensure that you don't end up just taking your old life and habits on the road, especially if they aren't working for you.

As you've seen, there are enormous variables associated with RV living, including expenses and how you choose to do it. You'll want to ask yourself some questions to gain clarity around your reasons, as these will help guide many of your other decisions involved in the research, prep, and planning stages and help you get clearer around the expenses as they relate to you and your goals.

THE ROCKS, PEBBLES, SAND EXERCISE

You may have heard of this one before, but if not, give it a try. Picture a large glass jar on a table. Now picture a pile of stones, a bag of pebbles, a bag of sand, and a glass of water. The challenge is to fill the jar with as many or as much of those things as possible. You must start with the large rocks first because if you start with anything else, the stones won't fit. Having the stones in first will allow pebbles, then sand, and then water to fill in the gaps between the larger items, making the most of the space available.

This is a great analogy for RVing and life in general. You need to place your biggest and most important priorities first, and then let the rest fit in around them.

What Is Your "Why"?

Whether you're planning to RV solo or as a couple or family, start by asking some questions about your reasons for wanting to do this, to define your top goals and priorities. The answers are going to be different for everyone, but it's important for you to understand your primary driving forces for wanting to live the RV lifestyle, because they will help you know what to focus on when creating your action plan and as you make decisions. Ask yourself:

What excites you most about living the RV life?

_____

_____

What is your primary financial goal while RVing—to save money, maintain your current financial status, or spend money?

_____

_____

What do you and your traveling companions want to experience together?

_____

_____

What places and people do you want to visit on your travels?

_____

_____

How social do you want your RV life to be?

_____

_____

What kinds of skills or experiences do you want to develop?

_____

_____

What do you want to change or improve in your life?

_____

_____

How do you imagine RVing will enhance your life?

How long do you see yourself doing this?

After you've hung up the keys, what do you want to look back on and know you have achieved through your RVing experience?

Your answers to these questions will have a very big impact on your approach to planning and preparation. We'll continue making references to this "why" exercise throughout the book to keep you on track in making the right decisions for you.

WHAT'S YOUR STYLE?

The better you know yourself, the better you'll be able to make decisions that support your values and priorities. Remember those big rocks in the jar we talked about earlier? When you plan and make decisions for your RV life based on what's most important to you (the big rocks), you'll be more likely to stay on track and not get swayed by less important things (the pebbles and grains of sand).

Consider the things that are important to you and ask questions like:

What's your style of RV travel? Are you a camper who likes the idea of staying out in nature and off the grid? Are you happy staying in average RV parks or more rustic campgrounds with only basic hookups? Or are you a glamper who prefers modern RV resorts with nice amenities and the ability to hook up to utilities?

Are you someone who is okay with an RV with the standard basic necessities, or do you require additional creature comforts and luxuries, like a washer/dryer, residential fridge, or heated floors?

_____

_____

Who will be traveling with you—spouse, kids, and pets?

_____

_____

Will you be working on the road?

_____

_____

Do you like to be on the go frequently or move slowly and take your time?

_____

_____

RV TERMS TO KNOW

glamping: A fusion of *glamour and camping*, glamping is a more luxurious style of camping that allows you to enjoy nature and the lifestyle without having to sacrifice creature comforts.

WHEN CAN YOU HIT THE ROAD?

Most people have existing responsibilities to consider, such as family, home, job, and finances. If you don't currently have work you can do remotely, you might first need to find a role that you can fulfill from anywhere. Perhaps your kids are at an age where it's not ideal to take them out and roadschool. Maybe you are a year or two from retirement and it makes more financial sense to wait. Or, if you're already burned out mentally, physically, or emotionally, it may be a higher priority for you to make a life change as soon as possible.

No matter what your life circumstances, you can probably find a way to make the RV life work for you. Take some time to think about your priorities and what is realistic for you and your current situation by asking these questions:

What is your ideal timeframe for hitting the road in your RV?

_____

Does your current job or financial situation support doing it now, or does it make more sense to wait?

_____

What responsibilities do you currently have, and can these be managed remotely?

_____

Are there ways you could change your current situation, such as your job, to do this sooner rather than later?

_____

Would it make more sense to ease your way into the RV life with occasional or part-time travel before going full-time?

_____

Whose needs must you consider when making this decision (e.g., spouse, kids, parents)?

_____

On what date do you plan to hit the road?

_____

SETTING A DATE TO BEGIN

Yes, that's right: you should set a date for beginning your RV life! There's nothing like a deadline to get you moving and to give you a sense of purpose and focus as you work toward what you really want.

We've met people who went from "regular" living to RV living in less than thirty days, and others who have spent ten or more years planning their dream. This timeline will be different for everyone and depends on how simple or complex your current life is. To give you an idea, it took about eight months for us to hit the road after we started seriously talking about RVing, and that felt like we were moving quickly!

It's probably a good idea to allow a year or so for all this to happen at a reasonable pace without stressing yourself out too much. Of course, if you have a house to sell and a lifetime of possessions to offload as you downsize, it could take a lot longer, but it's possible to do it faster too.

DON'T STRESS YOURSELF OUT

Keep in mind that this is also an emotional journey, and some folks may take longer than others to move through the steps. After all, you're changing your life, and this can get scary or overwhelming at times…but it's also exciting! Just know that there is no right or wrong way. It's your life, your journey, and YOU get to decide on the pace that works for you! This isn't a race, so don't feel like you have to rush it, but don't keep putting things off to the point where you never actually do it either. Try and find a comfortable place in between.

Decide on a realistic date that feels comfortable for you to drive off in your RV that keeps you motivated but doesn't make you feel stressed or overwhelmed. Planning is part of the journey, so you may as well enjoy it! Post your launch date in a place where you can see it every day—on a mirror, on the refrigerator, or in your car. There's even an app for that—create an "event" in the *Countdown* app to count down the days to your launch date and keep focused on your goal.

Having a deadline for your goal makes it real, so set a date and work toward that, but don't be afraid to make adjustments either, if you need to.

LIGHTENING YOUR LOAD: WHAT TO DO WITH ALL YOUR STUFF

Regardless of your RV lifestyle goals, you will almost certainly need to downsize your possessions. American society is very focused on consumerism and the constant accumulation of "stuff." Buy stuff, fill your home and basement with stuff, fill your garage with stuff, and maybe even fill a storage unit with more stuff. Stuff you never use and end up paying hundreds, if not thousands, of dollars a year for, and we'd bet you don't even remember what stuff is in there anymore! Don't worry; we've been there too—at least Julie has.

WHY I LOVE RVING

Freida, 71

FULL-TIME RVER SINCE NOVEMBER 2016

YouTube: RVFreeDa
Instagram: @rvfreedausa
Facebook: Rvfreeda

"I'm so inspired by the beauty of North America that my age will not stop me from exploring!"

THERE WAS A TIME AFTER MY HUSBAND PASSED WHEN I FELT there was no future for me. I had done it all. I had owned my own multimedia business for twenty years, raised my kids, had a great garden...what more could I do? I was done. Wow, was I wrong!

When my husband, Gene, passed in 2013 after forty-seven years of laughing and loving, I was devastated. I'd never thought about moving away from Anaheim, California, because I loved my garden (you can still see my old gardening videos on *YouTube* at RVFreeDa). But I watched some *YouTube* videos that inspired me to research the possibility of living full-time in an RV. In early 2016 I made the commitment, and by November 8 of that year I had sold my house and was living on the road. I was sixty-nine years old, traveling as a solo woman RVer.

I didn't get rid of everything before I left, though. My husband was an artist, and I was his muse. His art made me laugh, and there was a lot of it in our home. I could not and still haven't parted with all of it. I plan on taking my time to savor it until I'm ready. Other than that, I'm free from the stuff that tied me down.

With my love for gardening, I fantasized about a double-decker bus with a garden on the top deck. Haha, like that would work. My best friend's husband was a mechanic who had passed a year before my husband. They had a 28-foot 1993 Class A with 50,000 miles on it. She offered to sell it to me for $500 and was happy to get it out of the driveway. I invested $10,000 replacing aged parts and preparing it and the truck I tow behind it for the road, and took off with my two dogs—a German shepherd called Seesmic and my dachshund, Mikee.

I decided to celebrate my seventieth birthday (in 2017) in Seward, Alaska. So I drove up to Bellingham, Washington, boarded the ferry with my RV, and headed to Haines, Alaska. I had planned to go to northern Alaska, but the beauty of Seward overwhelmed me and I stayed there all summer. The camp host, Tim, and the friends I met there threw me a huge party on the beach of Resurrection Bay. It was amazing and the best birthday celebration I have ever had.

I started my return trip down the Alaska Highway in early fall of 2017, drove through Canada, and then headed to Tennessee to see my three grandkids and enjoy the holidays with them before returning to visit my friends in California after the best year of my life. And it was all because I discovered through all my RVing mentors on *YouTube* that I was NOT done yet! If your health is okay, then your age should never stop you. Fear that I was too old just about stopped me from having the best year of my life—and that was just the start. I want you to know that you are NOT DONE YET either!

You may not even realize just how big a part of your life this cycle of stuff is until you step off the treadmill and choose to live differently, like those of us who live in our RVs. Letting go of unnecessary stuff brings with it an amazing feeling of freedom and lightness that is hard to describe. It's like a weight is being lifted from your shoulders when you realize you really don't need all that stuff.

We've met some folks who are ruthless when it comes to getting rid of their possessions, but it's not always that easy for everyone. The purging process can be an emotional journey, especially if you're downsizing a home where you've raised a family and lived for decades. We'll talk more about the emotional side of downsizing in Chapter 4, but for now let's focus on the practical side of downsizing as it relates to planning and preparation for your RV life. Starting today, you're going to pretend you're already an RVer anytime you go shopping, as part of your training!

What You Will Need in Your RV

Some of what you already own might also be useful in your RV. Following is an overview of the most important things you'll need, which will help you focus on offloading the rest. Remember, your RV will be much more limited on space, and you may even decide to switch out some existing items for others that are more compact, lightweight, or multipurpose. For example, we sold our blender, food processor, and juicer in a yard sale and replaced them with a Ninja food-prep system that does it all (or close enough for our needs).

These are the most important items you'll need with you in your RV:

- ☐ Your computer, tablet, and work equipment
- ☐ Cameras and electronics
- ☐ Key kitchen items (e.g., coffee maker, multiuse appliance, a few cooking pans, bowls)
- ☐ Dishes and silverware—we find that a setting for four is plenty for the two of us (Corelle works well, as it's fairly lightweight and not too bulky)
- ☐ Coffee mugs and wine glasses—we recently switched to a colorful set of stemless, stainless-steel tumblers that can be used for hot or cold beverages and are great for both indoor and outdoor use
- ☐ Clothing and shoes that you wear often and will be suitable for a more casual lifestyle and the weather you'll be spending most of your time in
- ☐ Personal care items (e.g., shaver, toothbrush, toiletries, makeup)

- [ ] Sheets and towels—one or two sets is usually plenty
- [ ] Only very special or necessary books, such as educational resources if you'll be roadschooling kids—books are heavy, so resist the temptation to take too many, and start getting used to buying your books digitally, like ebooks or audiobooks
- [ ] Basic tools, such as a few screwdrivers, an adjustable wrench, a tape measure, pliers, and a small hammer—the rest you can buy from a local store as needed or borrow from a fellow RVer

These are the things you really need for everyday living. You won't need nearly as many kitchen utensils as you currently have, and you really only need one of most things. Focus on multipurpose items that make your life simpler—do you really need an egg slicer and an ice cream scoop when you have a knife and a spoon?

And remember, you're traveling the country, not going to Mars, so if you ever find you really do need something that you offloaded or left in storage, you can always buy it again or borrow it on the road. You'll never be far from what you may need.

STOP BRINGING STUFF IN

First, you need to break the unconscious pattern of buying stuff whenever you feel like it to stop the accumulation. Most RVers follow the rule that whenever something comes into the RV, something has to go out. This helps keep your life filled with what really matters and prevents you from falling into mindless consumerism. It also helps prevent your RV from becoming cluttered and overweight, which can become a safety hazard, cause conflict, or add to your stress.

When you're out shopping, before mindlessly putting items into your cart, stop and ask yourself, "Would this make sense to buy if I was already living in my RV?" Think about what you would need to give up to bring that item in. You can also stop buying in bulk, as you just won't need or have the space for a gallon-sized jug of mayonnaise or twenty-pound bag of rice. Break, or at least curb, your shopping habits starting now. If you previously bought in bulk, you can start living off your stockpiles to downsize your pantry and get into the habit of shopping like an RVer. Buy smaller amounts at a time and you'll probably find it will actually save you money, which you can put toward your RVing goals.

BREAK DOWN THE TASK INTO SMALLER CHUNKS

It's not easy to look at everything in your home and immediately know what should stay and what should go. But most people will be moving from a home of 1,500–3,500 square feet into a home on wheels that is around 150–350 square feet, about one-tenth of the size! The simple physics means you will need to find new homes for most of your stuff.

When Julie moved from Australia to the US, she could bring only two suitcases on the plane. While she did leave some things in storage at her mother's house, she had to fit her most important, favorite items into those two suitcases. Having a space limitation really helps you prioritize the most important and favorite things you want to bring with you—practical items you use the most, and things that make you happy. You simply don't have room for stuff you don't absolutely love and use often, so start getting clear on what those items are and be willing to let the rest go.

This can be a big and overwhelming exercise, so pace yourself and break it down into smaller chunks, like by room or by type of item. This exercise can get exhausting, and the more tired you get, the harder it is to be ruthless. You can set aside a whole day here and there to make a big dent, but we recommend starting small and doing a little bit every day to make it more manageable. For example, dedicate fifteen to twenty minutes a day to a specific area, like a kitchen cabinet, desk drawer, or small linen closet. Set a reminder alarm on your phone for your daily downsizing date, put on some upbeat music, start the timer, and dive in! You'll start seeing results immediately, feel inspired and energized while you do it, and be amazed by how much progress you can make in a short time.

HOW TO SORT THROUGH YOUR STUFF

As you take stock of what you own, try to get rid of things that you don't use or that don't bring you joy. Divide your stuff into three categories as you work:

1. Must-haves—things you can't live without and use daily or often
2. Can live without—things that are important to you but that you don't often use
3. Replaceable—things you might be able to change out for others that will work better

When you are really honest with yourself, you'll soon realize that there are very few things you use every day that are true must-haves.

Here are some more tips for going through your items:

- **Garage/shed:** Start in your garage or shed—you won't need that lawn mower, rake, or snow shovel in your RV! However, small maintenance tools, like screwdrivers and pliers, will come in handy on the road.

- **Kitchen appliances:** Go through your kitchen and choose your very favorite items and keep them on the counter or in a single, easy-access cupboard. Remove items you hardly ever use, like specific-use appliances, from the kitchen entirely and put any remaining items on difficult-to-reach shelves. Making them less accessible will reduce your tendency to use them and show how well you can function with a more limited set of kitchen items. You might even stop using the dishwasher if you don't plan on having one in your RV.

- **Dishes and cups:** You'll find you don't need nearly as many dishes and cups as you think. We know people with more than twenty coffee cups in their homes, and they may use a dozen before running the dishwasher. When you wash dishes by hand, you will likely find that you need only one or two cups and plates per person, as you wash them every time you use them in an RV. We travel with service for four, which has served us well. When entertaining larger groups, we use disposable plates and cutlery.

What to Do with Your Stuff

You'll want to create four piles for the things that are deemed Can Live Withouts or Replaceables so you can:

- ☐ **Sell it:** Selling your stuff is a great way to downsize and make money to fund your RV life. Keep a box or pile in the basement or garage until you've amassed everything you want to sell. Then sell items on *Craigslist*, *letgo*, *Decluttr*, *Facebook Marketplace*, or *eBay*; organize a yard sale; or hire an estate company to take care of everything.

- ☐ **Give it away:** There will be things that are important to you that you don't use often at all, such as heirlooms, specialized cookware, clothing, and sporting equipment. While some of these items might make it into your RV, they may also find new homes with family or friends who will enjoy them. Put the items you want to give to family or friends into boxes and take them to the garage or basement for now.

☐ **Donate it:** There are lots of ways to donate your belongings. One fun idea is to host a "housecooling party"—the opposite of a housewarming party! Invite family, friends, and neighbors to take what they want. Offer them drinks to help empty your liquor cabinet at the same time. You can also list items on *Freecycle* for people to come and collect. Of course, you can also donate to Goodwill or other charities/thrift stores—be sure to get a receipt for your taxes! Put items for donation into big trash bags or boxes and place them in the back of your car to drop off next time you're near a thrift store or donation center.

☐ **Trash it:** Dispose of trash and recycling as you go.

You will be surprised how good it will feel to lighten your load, and of course, the money you make from selling stuff will come in very handy for your RV life. We heard of a woman who made so much money selling all her stuff that she bought her RV with the proceeds!

WHAT ABOUT STORAGE?

Of course, there's also the option of storing stuff you just can't bear to part with, and many RVers do keep a small storage unit when they first hit the road full-time, but when they return, they usually end up purging most of it anyway. Unless you are planning to RV for a limited period of time, we encourage you to try and pare down as much as you can and store just a few keepsakes in a small box with a family member or friend. Otherwise, you'll just be wasting money storing stuff you won't end up wanting or needing.

Also, something to keep in mind—if you offer heirlooms, photographs, and special items to family and friends and they don't want them now, it's likely they never will, so don't spend money storing them!

DIGITIZING YOUR PAPERWORK AND PHOTOS

A very handy tip is to start digitizing important documents, records, and photographs. You can use a regular scanner or even an app like TurboScan on your smartphone for scanning documents. You can also use special photo-scanning machines or outsource the task to companies that specialize in digitizing your photo and video memories. (It may cost money, but it will save you time, and the quality will likely be better.) Store your digital files on a hard drive and keep a backup in a safety deposit box or with a trusted family member.

You can also take all your photos or videos with you on a hard drive or play the photos on a digital photo frame. If you have a favorite piece of artwork that you love looking at each day, take a photo and print a smaller version of it that you can frame and hang in your RV. If you're having trouble letting go of some favorite artwork or trinkets, take photos of them too. Studies have shown that photographs of an item can evoke many of the same emotions as seeing the actual item in person.

NEXT STEPS

Now that you have defined your goals, created a budget, planned your launch date, and started downsizing, you should have a good idea of what areas you need to focus on and the timeframe you have to do it in. You may choose to divide and conquer the tasks with your partner, or you may be leading the way. Just create a framework for your RV life plan to keep you on track, and ensure you're covering all the bases. Now it's time to look into finding your RV!

CHAPTER 3

FINDING YOUR HOME ON WHEELS

Choosing the Right RV Setup for You

"Finding the right RV—especially one you plan to spend a lot of time with—is a bit like trying to find the right person to marry. When you take your time, are clear on what you want, and wait until you find 'the right one,' it makes all the difference, and the journey will be a lot more enjoyable."

—*Marc Bennett, coauthor of this book*

There's a lot to learn about RVs—the different types, what features are important, how they work, and how to take care of them. Choosing an RV can be fairly simple if you're using it only occasionally, but if you're planning to RV full-time or for extended periods, you'll need to weigh what features are most important to you in order to find the one that will best fit your needs. We have literally written the equivalent of an entire book on this topic in our online course "Choosing the Right RV for You" (visit www.rvsuccessschool.com to take it), but in this chapter we'll provide a good overview of the options, as well as RV safety, systems, and maintenance. What you learn here will put you ahead of many RV shoppers and improve your chances of finding the right RV for your lifestyle so you can focus on traveling and enjoying your adventures!

WHAT ARE THE DIFFERENT TYPES OF RVS?

CLASS A—MOTORHOME OR BUS CONVERSION

- Usually looks like a bus and ranges in size from 26' to 45' in length; also known as coach or motor coach

- Has a relatively large living area, often with additional slideouts

- Easy access to living space while on the road

- Good storage inside and outside

- May have a toy hauler/garage option for large items

- Built on a specially designed chassis (some heavier chassis allow for more luxurious features, such as tiled floors, porcelain toilets, solid wood cabinetry, and larger fuel and holding tanks)

- Some may feel intimidated driving it because of the size

- Larger Class As may require a special license

- Can be powered by gas or diesel

- Lowest fuel economy, usually 6–10 mpg

- Bus conversions range from an old-school bus to a luxury motorcoach

- Height typically up to 13'6"; weight can vary up to around 50,000 lbs

- New prices range from $60,000 to well over $2 million

CLASS B—MOTORHOME

- This is basically a van that has been converted into an RV, has an elevated roof, and ranges from 17' to 24' in length

- Can be Class B or B+ (B+ is slightly larger in height/width)

- Highly maneuverable, easy to drive, some have off-road capability

- Can be powered by gas or diesel

- Good gas mileage; around 12–25 mpg

- Easy access to living space while on the road

- Minimal storage inside and outside

- Can be tight living space for more than one person long term

- Height typically up to 10'; weight can vary up to 12,000 lbs

- New prices range from $40,000 to more than $200,000

There are Class As, Class Bs, Class B+s, Class Cs, Class Super Cs, fifth wheels, travel trailers, toy haulers, and truck campers. Does that sound like a lot to consider? Don't worry; we'll break it all down for you. Let's take a look at the different types to understand some of their features, pros, and cons.

CLASS A

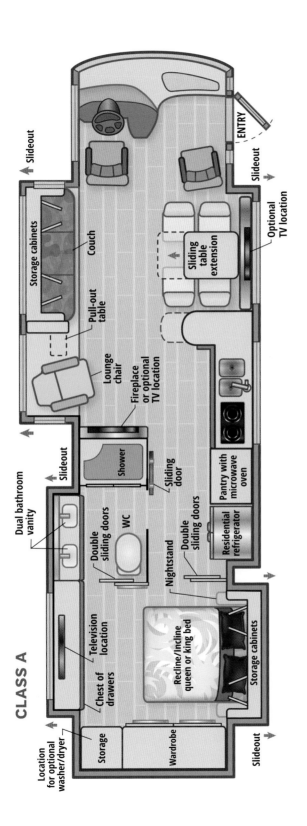

- Slideout
- Storage cabinets
- Couch
- Slideout
- ENTRY
- Pull-out table
- Sliding table extension
- Optional TV location
- Lounge chair
- Fireplace or optional TV location
- Slideout
- Slideout
- Dual bathroom vanity
- Shower
- Sliding door
- Pantry with microwave oven
- Double sliding doors
- WC
- Nightstand
- Double sliding doors
- Residential refrigerator
- Television location
- Chest of drawers
- Recline/Incline queen or king bed
- Storage cabinets
- Location for optional washer/dryer
- Storage
- Wardrobe
- Slideout

CLASS B

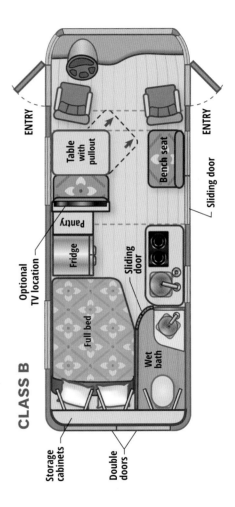

- ENTRY
- Table with pullout
- Bench seat
- ENTRY
- Sliding door
- Optional TV location
- Pantry
- Fridge
- Sliding door
- Full bed
- Wet bath
- Storage cabinets
- Double doors

WHAT ARE THE DIFFERENT TYPES OF RVS?

CLASS C—MOTORHOME

- The most common type of rental RVs, consisting of a van chassis with a home box built on it, range from 22' to 35' in length

- Budget-friendly cost makes it an entry-level motorhome

- Easy to drive and maneuver

- Built on a regular automotive chassis

- Can be powered by gas or diesel

- Has an over-cab bed, which may be the only bed or extra sleeping quarters

- Easy access to living space while on the road

- Still relatively small and maneuverable, but with more living space and storage space than a similar length Class B

- Gas mileage between 8–20 mpg

- Height typically up to 11'; weight can vary, up to 15,000 lbs

- New prices range from $50,000 to more than $150,000

CLASS SUPER C—MOTORHOME

- A much heavier-duty version of a Class C motorhome powered by a larger diesel truck engine and cab; ranges from 35' to 45' in length

- Heavier chassis, larger size, more storage, and higher cargo-carrying and towing capacities

- Average fuel economy, usually 8–12 mpg

- Easy access to living space while on the road

- Higher price than regular Class Cs

- Higher-end units can be as luxurious as some Class A motorhomes

- Height typically up to 13'6"; weight can vary, up to 50,000 lbs

- New prices range from $160,000 to well over $500,000

CLASS C

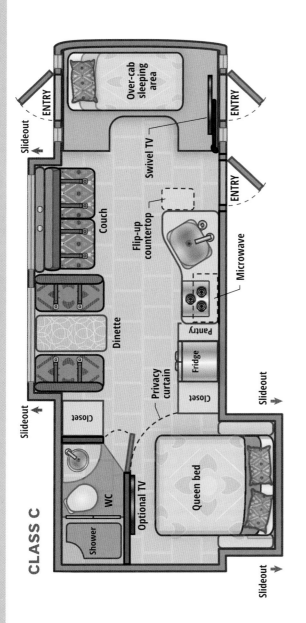

Slideout
ENTRY
Slideout
Closet
Shower
WC
Optional TV
Privacy curtain
Closet
Fridge
Pantry
Microwave
Flip-up countertop
Swivel TV
Couch
Dinette
Queen bed
ENTRY
ENTRY
Over-cab sleeping area
Slideout
Slideout

CLASS SUPER C

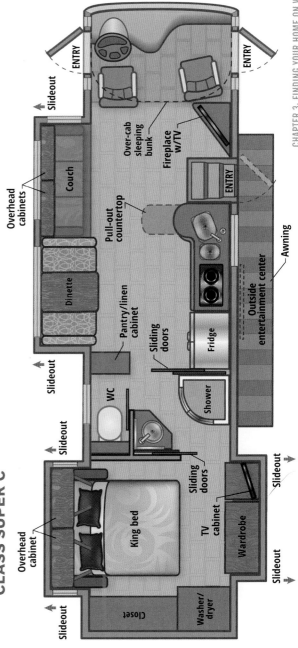

Slideout
Slideout
Overhead cabinets
Couch
Dinette
Pantry/linen cabinet
Sliding doors
WC
Overhead cabinet
King bed
Sliding doors
TV cabinet
Wardrobe
Washer/dryer
Closet
Slideout
Slideout
Slideout
Slideout
Fridge
Shower
Outside entertainment center
Awning
Pull-out countertop
Over-cab sleeping bunk
Fireplace w/TV
ENTRY
ENTRY
ENTRY
Slideout

WHAT ARE THE DIFFERENT TYPES OF RVS?

FIFTH WHEEL—TOWABLE

- Largest type of towable RV; can range from 19' to 45' in length—often larger than the truck towing it

- Must have a pickup with open bed to tow one—larger fifth wheels may require a dually

- Very livable and the most "home-like" of RVs

- Usually more inside storage and basement storage than other towables

- Height typically up to 13'; weight can vary, from 4,000 to over 30,000 lbs

- New prices range from $20,000 to well over $200,000

TRAVEL TRAILER—TOWABLE

- Traditional trailer that attaches to a hitch at the rear of the tow vehicle; usually 16' to 35' in length

- The most common and affordable towable RV, with a lower entry cost than a fifth wheel

- Huge variety of sizes and styles

- Lighter weight and less expensive versions may skimp on quality, as they're intended more for vacation and weekends than full-time living

- Depending on size, can be towed with passenger car, SUV, or large truck; some can be very off-road capable

- Height typically up to 11'; weight usually varies from 1,500 to 11,000 lbs

- New prices generally range from $6,000 to $60,000 but can exceed $200,000 for some luxury and custom models

FIFTH WHEEL

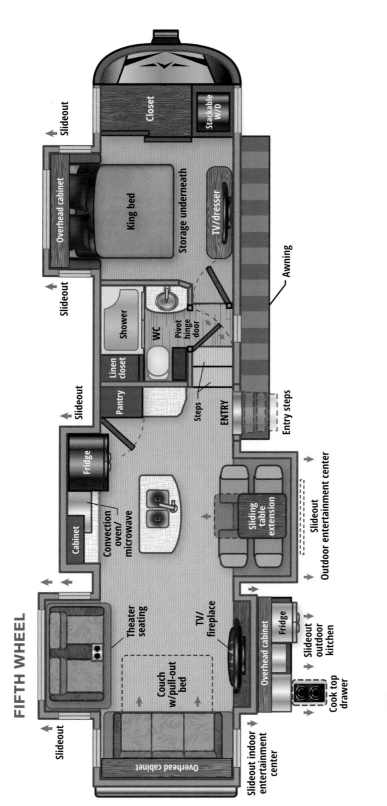

Slideout

Slideout

Overhead cabinet

Closet

Stackable W/D

King bed

Storage underneath

TV/dresser

Awning

Shower

WC

Linen closet

Pantry

Pivot hinge door

Steps

ENTRY

Entry steps

Slideout

Fridge

Cabinet

Convection oven/microwave

Sliding table extension

Slideout Outdoor entertainment center

Theater seating

TV/fireplace

Couch w/pull-out bed

Overhead cabinet

Fridge

Slideout outdoor kitchen

Cook top drawer

Slideout indoor entertainment center

Overhead cabinet

Slideout

TRAVEL TRAILER

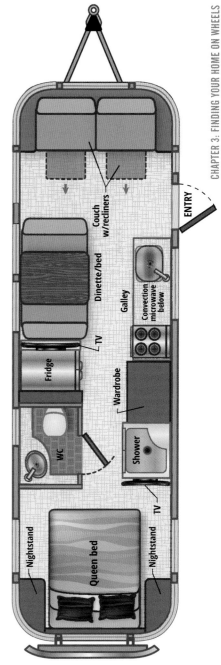

Couch w/recliners

Dinette/bed

Galley

Convection microwave below

ENTRY

TV

Fridge

Wardrobe

WC

Shower

TV

Nightstand

Queen bed

Nightstand

WHAT ARE THE DIFFERENT TYPES OF RVS?

TOY HAULER–TOWABLE

- Travel trailers or fifth wheel with garage to carry large items like toys, bikes, golf carts, motorcycles, and other sporting equipment; usually 30'–45' in length

- Garage can double as a second room or office when not hauling items

- If not using the garage as living space, you sacrifice living space for empty garage when parked

- Towed with a truck or other vehicle with large tow capacity

- Height typically from 11' to 13'; weight can vary from 10,000 to 25,000 lbs

- New prices generally range from $10,000 to $140,000

TRUCK CAMPER

- Any RV that can be carried in the bed of a pickup truck; also known as a slide-in or over-cab, typically 15'–20' in length

- Highly maneuverable and good for off-roading, can go anywhere the truck can go

- Can be mounted in your existing truck, and is easily removable

- Generally a very small but efficient living space

- Generally doesn't require registration and is insured with your truck

- Height typically up to 9' (3'–4' above truck cab); weighs 1,200–4,000 lbs

- New prices can range from $8,000 to over $50,000

TOY HAULER

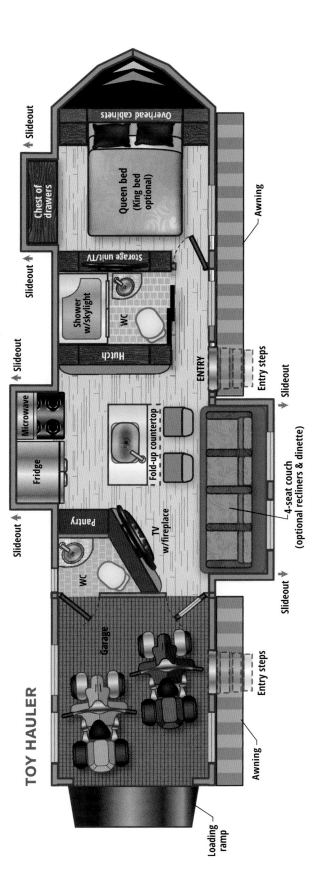

- Slideout
- Slideout
- Chest of drawers
- Overhead cabinets
- Queen bed (King bed optional)
- Storage unit/TV
- Shower w/skylight
- WC
- Hutch
- Slideout
- Microwave
- Fridge
- Fold-up countertop
- Slideout
- Pantry
- WC
- TV w/fireplace
- Garage
- Entry steps
- Awning
- ENTRY
- Entry steps
- Slideout
- 4-seat couch (optional recliners & dinette)
- Slideout
- Awning
- Loading ramp

TRUCK CAMPER

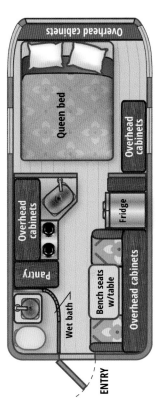

- Overhead cabinets
- Queen bed
- Overhead cabinets
- Overhead cabinets
- Fridge
- Pantry
- Bench seats w/table
- Overhead cabinets
- Wet bath
- ENTRY

WHICH RVS ARE DESIGNED FOR FULL-TIME LIVING?

The most common choices of RVs for full-time living tend to be Class A motorhomes and fifth wheels, but there are also plenty of RVers who live full-time in travel trailers, Class B or Class C motorhomes, vans, or even truck campers. It's all a matter of personal taste and budget, and there really is an RV out there for everyone, including those looking for serious off-road capability.

When considering RVs for full-time living, the key features to look for are quality construction and insulation, floor plan, and reliability. Most RVs are built for the purpose of occasional weekend recreation, not regular daily use, so pay attention to important things for day-to-day living, like comfort, convenience, space, and storage.

WHERE TO START LOOKING FOR RVS

Now that you have a general understanding of the many different kinds of RVs available, you'll want to go and see them in person to get a sense of which ones feel most comfortable to you.

A good place to start your RV shopping is an RV show, where they will have the biggest range of RV types, sizes, styles, and price points. But remember, most of these will be new, and you don't have to buy new. Keep in mind that the prices given in this book are for new RVs, and you can buy a used RV of any kind for just about any price, depending on age, type, and condition. You can also visit your local RV dealer, where they will have a selection of both new and used RVs, to get an idea of what's available used. RVs are usually advertised with the MSRP (manufacturer's suggested retail price), which is rarely the price you'll end up paying, so just consider the MSRP as a very general guide for now.

PLEASE promise yourself and us that you WILL NOT buy an RV on your first visit—no matter how excited you get when you think you've found "the one"! This isn't a decision to be made hastily, especially when you're still in the learning phase.

Download our handy RV Shopper Checklist at https://rvlove.com/book-bonus-content to use as a guide.

RV TERMS TO KNOW

campervan: In Australia, New Zealand, and the UK, motorhomes are also often referred to as campervans.

caravan: In Australia, New Zealand, and the UK, travel trailers are usually called caravans. In North America, caravan is a term used for a group of RVers traveling together.

slide-on: Australian term for truck campers.

demountable or dismountable: In the UK and Europe, truck campers are referred to as demountable or dismountable.

THE MOST IMPORTANT CONSIDERATIONS IN BUYING AN RV: FLOOR PLAN AND QUALITY CONSTRUCTION

In real estate it's about location, but in RVs you can change your location whenever you choose, so it's about floor plan/layout, and quality! Let's look into those topics in more detail.

FLOOR PLAN/LAYOUT

When you visit an RV show or dealer, pay attention to the floor plan and layout of RVs and think about how they could work for your lifestyle. How are the living area, kitchen, bedroom, and bathroom? Is there a decent space to work from if you plan to work on the road? What about storage? What are the capacities of the holding tanks for water, waste, and fuel? Consider each area of the RVs as you narrow down your choices. For example:

- If you like watching TV, ensure that the TV is located in front of the couch and not mounted on a sidewall, forcing you to look sideways to watch it.

- If you plan on cooking most meals in your RV, make sure the kitchen has enough counter space for food preparation, and space around the sink for doing dishes.

- If you plan on working from your RV, look for a comfortable place where you can work for extended periods or easily modify for your needs.

- If you plan to live in your RV full-time, will you want to convert that sofa to a bed and vice versa every day? Or is it important to have an RV with a separate sofa and bed?

- If you need to get up in the middle of the night, consider whether the bed layout allows you to do so without crawling over your partner.

For us it was important to find an RV with workspaces that didn't affect the primary living areas, which is why we bought an RV with a bedroom plus a separate bunk bed area that we converted to a dedicated office for Marc to work from.

Look at the RV with the slides extended, and then retract the slides on the RV to ensure that you will still be able to access important places, like the bathroom and fridge, on travel days.

These ideas may all sound simple or obvious, but you'd be surprised how many people don't think this through and end up changing their RVs after a short time because the layout doesn't work for them. Changing RVs can become a very expensive exercise, so it literally pays to think these things through! If you keep your RV for a while, you can reduce the financial impact and live a life of full-time travel for less than what your traditional life costs.

TEST BEFORE YOU BUY

When you've found an RV that you think could work for you, spend time in it (without the salesperson) and pretend you are living in it. Pretend you are accessing cupboards, taking a shower, preparing meals, doing dishes, working on your laptop, watching TV, getting ready for bed, and even sitting on the toilet. Remember, you're just pretending! While an RV layout might look good at first glance, when you pay closer attention, you may find that some aspects are difficult to live with. So what kinds of difficulties could there be?

- You may find you can't lift up your arms in the shower to wash your hair without bumping the walls.

- You may not be able to use your dominant hand when taking care of business on the toilet because it's so close to the wall that there's little to no room to move.

- In some smaller RVs, like Class Bs, you may find that you can't even open the fridge door while the bed is down..

These may be only minor inconveniences for weekend trips, but they could present a huge problem when trying to live in your RV full-time. Fortunately, there are hundreds of different floor plans available to fit your specific needs, including fully wheelchair-accessible RVs with lift gates for those with limited mobility. Truly, there are so many RVs out there, you're bound to find one that works for you; it may just take a little time. Or you could get lucky and find the right one soon after you start looking.

If you are buying a motorhome, you will want to take it for a test drive first to ensure that you are comfortable driving it. It may be nerve-racking at first, but you can always take RV driving lessons to increase your confidence and ability.

UNDERSTANDING RV QUALITY AND RELIABILITY

RVs are not built like cars. Auto manufacturers use high levels of engineering, automation, and precision manufacturing accompanied by high levels of quality control. On the other hand, RVs are mostly built by hand in relatively low-tech facilities, and the RV industry is not as heavily regulated as the automotive industry. The way RVs are built, combined with the complexity of the unit and the fact that RVs are subjected to the additional stressors of driving on all kinds of road conditions and surfaces, means it's like your home goes through an earthquake every time you drive it. Contrary to what you might expect, buying a new RV—even an expensive one—doesn't mean it will be perfect and free of issues. In fact, virtually every RV will have what's often called a "seasoning" or "breaking-in" period, where the first owner needs to work through the issues, bugs, and fixes to get everything in full working order. When you drive a new car off the lot, it is usually trouble-free for some time, but an RV rarely is. It may seem counterintuitive, but a used or preowned RV that has been well taken care of can often be more reliable, less expensive, and require fewer repairs than a brand-new RV, as the previous owner (hopefully) will have worked out the issues during the breaking-in period. Of course, this depends on how well the previous owner(s) took care of and maintained the RV and the initial build quality. Most RVs come with only a one-year limited factory warranty, so as a new buyer you'll need to get right onto those fixes if you want them to be covered by the manufacturer within the warranty period.

BUYING YOUR RV

An RV can be one of the largest purchases you'll ever make, so research and consider each option carefully to ensure you are making a good choice. It's easy to overspend, especially if you are an uninformed buyer and pay full retail price or simply make a poor decision. The MSRP in the RV industry has become a bit of a joke. You've probably seen cars on sale at a dealership for substantially less than the MRSP (say, 10 percent), but it's common to be able to buy a brand-new RV for 15, 20, or even 30 percent off the MSRP, depending on a range of circumstances that can be frustratingly inconsistent. An RV will also depreciate the minute you drive it off a dealer's lot, so understand that if you pay the full MSRP, you will immediately be upside-down in the value of your RV by 20 percent or more. That can add up to big bucks fast. When you go to trade in your RV, the numbers get even worse, as dealers will offer you only a fraction of the value you might be able to get on the private retail market. But trading in is more convenient, so some RV owners will just roll that shortfall into another loan on their next RV, further burying themselves in debt and kicking the financial can down the road. This is just another reason why it pays to take your time, do your homework, and find the right RV for you.

THINK ABOUT WHAT YOU CURRENTLY DRIVE

One of the best ways to start figuring out what type of RV might suit your needs is to look at what you currently drive. If you already own a big truck or SUV, then a towable RV could make the most sense. One of the biggest expenses related to buying a towable RV is that you'll also need to buy a vehicle capable of towing it. Trucks built to tow big fifth wheels often cost over $60,000 when new. Plus, you'll need to be comfortable driving that tow vehicle as your primary mode of transport when not towing the RV. If you already regularly drive something like that, you're ahead of the game financially and in terms of driving comfort.

A smaller towable RV might require only an SUV or lighter-duty vehicle to tow it. Just be sure to carefully match your towable RV with a suitably rated vehicle that is capable of towing the RV weight (including contents) safely.

If, on the other hand, you do most of your driving in a regular passenger vehicle, you may prefer to buy a motorized RV and plan on towing a car.

Another common path is to sell everything you currently have and purchase a single motorized RV that will serve as your only vehicle. This works great if you plan to travel frequently and are doing so on a tighter budget. You could carry

an electric bike or a small motorcycle to run errands and explore with. If you choose to tow a car behind a motorized RV, depending on the car, you might opt to tow it on a trailer, on a tow dolly, or with all four of the car's wheels on the ground (often called flat towing or four-down). You will need to carefully research this to find out which is the best option for you and your vehicle. We have some additional information and resources on this topic available at https://rvlove.com/book-bonus-content.

Remember, you can create whatever RV lifestyle you want—there is a virtually endless list of options. It's all about finding the option that works best for YOU.

RV TERMS TO KNOW

depreciation: The diminishing value of an RV (or any vehicle) over time due to aging, mileage, and wear and tear.

factory warranty: The period during which the manufacturer covers repairs on a new RV—usually one year (sometimes two).

extended service contract: Also called an extended warranty, this covers certain repairs on your new or used RV outside of the factory warranty period to help you control costs.

inspection: A thorough check of an RV, systems, and mechanicals, usually prepurchase, to ensure there are no major issues with the RV, or to identify areas of concern.

Should You Buy New or Used?

While there were more than 500,000 new RVs manufactured in the US in 2017, a high percentage of RV sales are actually preowned units, largely because used RVs are more affordable, but also because gently used RVs can often be less trouble than new units. Let's look at the benefits of each.

BENEFITS TO BUYING NEW

- You'll know the entire history of the RV and how it was taken care of.
- You can be assured that it won't have seen any pets (especially important if you're allergic).
- It will come with the manufacturer's warranty for the first year (or two years in some cases).
- You can often choose your desired colors and options.

BENEFITS TO BUYING A PREOWNED RV

- You'll save money by avoiding the initial, bigger depreciation hit (though depreciation will usually continue).
- The previous owner may have discovered and fixed any bugs during the seasoning period.
- You can choose from many years' worth of inventory, and it's common to be able to buy a higher-quality, older RV for a similar price to that of a lower-quality, newer RV.

WHERE TO BUY YOUR RV

Most RV dealers tend to carry both new and used inventory, but there are many other places to shop for RVs online that will help educate you and give you a feel for what's out there. In fact, there are more places to buy RVs than you probably realize, such as:

- RV dealers
- RV shows
- Websites like RVTrader.com and RVT.com
- Owners' groups for particular brands in online forums
- Online marketplaces like *Craigslist* and *eBay*
- Your local newspaper
- RV-related magazines
- Ads posted on community boards in RV parks and campgrounds
- RV manufacturers that sell direct from the factory to consumers
- Friends and family or local community—a lot of RVs are actually found through word of mouth and sold privately, so keep an ear to the ground. You never know what might come along once you start paying attention! The advantage of buying an RV from someone you know or a private party is you get to learn a lot more about its usage, care, and maintenance history.

Before you make your purchase, you can get ratings, in-depth reviews of RV quality, and information on how RVs are built at RVReviews.net. And you can research RVs, floor plans, and brands at manufacturer websites and sites like RVingPlanet.com.

SHOULD YOU RENT AN RV BEFORE BUYING?

If you aren't sure whether RVing is for you or what kind of RV might suit you best, consider renting an RV (or even two or three) before making a big purchase. Renting an RV will allow you to work out which RV types, floor plans, and features are most important to you and how you will travel. The cost of an RV rental may seem high at first, but when you consider the many thousands you will likely spend (or potentially waste) on an RV purchase, it could end up being a wise investment.

There are several avenues for renting other types of RVs besides the big-name Class C rentals you'll often see driving around national parks and popular tourist areas. There are websites like RVshare.com and Outdoorsy.com, where you'll find private RV owners willing to rent out their RVs, and you may even find an RV to rent that is similar to the type you eventually plan on purchasing. Some RV dealerships offer rental RVs, too, and may even apply the rental costs toward the purchase of a vehicle from their store.

RV FINANCING

When you're ready to buy your RV, you may be able to get ten- or even twenty-year financing, depending on your credit and the bank you want to use. Not all banks will finance RVs, and even fewer banks will finance RVs for full-time RVers, so this is an area where you will really need to do your homework well in advance of making any large decisions, such as buying your RV or selling your home. Compare banks, rates, and terms, and even try to get your RV financing preapproved before making your purchase. Your chances of being approved and getting a good rate may be better if you still own property and/or have a physical residence.

RVs that contain sleeping, bathroom, and kitchen facilities are generally allowed to be financed more like homes than cars, and the interest paid on an RV loan is often tax deductible just like home mortgage interest. If you plan on financing your RV purchase, be aware that while your RV may be eligible for a long-term loan, financing on a truck or other tow vehicle is usually limited to seven years. Sometimes a towing vehicle (truck) can cost more than the RV it tows. Be cautious when considering long-term financing, as RVs are generally depreciating assets, consistently losing value year after year.

One final comment on purchasing is that it pays to do your research in advance. Most RV dealers offer financing, which is convenient, and they may offer a competitive rate, but you won't know if it's a good deal unless you know the going market rates. Being preapproved for RV financing can also improve your negotiating position, so know your options before you commit to making a large purchase.

UNDERSTANDING DEPRECIATION

Long-term loans on traditional homes are generally safer for lenders, as historically they tend to be appreciating assets that allow for the value to offset the cost of the interest on the loan over the years. This is not the case with RVs, so be sure to factor in the estimated effects of RV depreciation when creating your budget, knowing that the steepest decline will be in the first couple of years.

It is not uncommon for RVs to depreciate 10 percent year over year, so paying interest on a long-term loan will leave you more and more upside down in the purchase every year. At some point you will need to pay the difference—whether you put down a large deposit up front, pay extra on your monthly payments, or pay the difference at the end is your decision.

Here's an example: in 2014 we paid $93,000 (plus taxes) for our first RV, which we bought used from a private seller when it was two years old (when new, the MSRP was around $130,000 plus taxes). We took out a twenty-year loan with a monthly payment of $570, and four years later we sold the RV privately for $75,000. We divided the loss of $25,000 by 48 to determine our approximate monthly depreciation, which came to about $520 per month. Keep in mind that that was on top of our $570 monthly RV loan payment. Ouch! But when it comes to RVs, this actually isn't considered too bad—it can often be much, much worse, especially if you buy a new or high-end RV. The way we look at our RV payment is in terms of the loan amount plus anticipated depreciation to better estimate our actual monthly cost, which for us, ended up being more like $1,100. Yes, that's a lot of money, but it's still around half of our previous mortgage, HOA fees, and other home-ownership related expenses, and we've had an incredible, life-changing experience while exploring the whole country. For us it was worth it, as it aligned with our own "why"—to experience more freedom, health, and travel.

In 2018 we bought our second RV, a twenty-year-old, high-end (in its day) motorhome, taking out a $35,000 seven-year loan with payments of $500 per month. When new, the MSRP was around $230,000, or about $346,000 in today's dollars. This RV has pretty much hit the bottom of its depreciation curve, so the financial impact of depreciation on our second RV will likely be much lower than on our first. We share our examples simply to illustrate a point about the impact of depreciation; you should not rely on these numbers as a guide when doing your RV budgeting, as there truly are so many variables. This is another area where you need to do your homework to get at least some idea of what to expect.

RV INSPECTIONS

If you're buying a preowned RV, you may want to consider having a professional inspection done, just as you would have a home inspected when buying real estate. A professional RV inspector (you can find one through PremierRVInspections.com)—or even a very experienced and thorough RV technician—should be able to catch any significant issues, identify areas for price negotiation on items that need repair or replacement, and provide peace of mind before buying. Be aware that there is no guarantee they will catch everything and you may still discover some issues down the track. However, we believe that having a professional RV inspection is a very worthwhile investment for just about any RV purchase to help reduce the risk of unexpected surprises and hassles down the road.

EXTENDED SERVICE CONTRACT

One of the main reasons people like buying new RVs is for the factory warranty. You can also buy an extended warranty (also known as an extended service contract) for most preowned RVs. If you decide to buy an extended service contract, do your research and get a quote in advance from a broker like WholesaleWarranties.com instead of just going with the policy offered by the RV dealer, as these are often marked up heavily. Contrary to how it may seem, an "exclusionary" policy covers far more than an "inclusionary" policy as it offers the highest level of coverage. Under an exclusionary warranty, every component on your RV will be covered, except for those items specifically listed under the "What Is Not Covered" section of the policy. This makes the coverage easy to understand, as you need only refer to the list of exclusions. Depending on your needs, an "inclusionary policy" may still make sense, but know that an exclusionary policy usually covers more. There are so many components in an RV that can break that you may not even be aware of, so an extended service contract can often be a worthwhile investment to help mitigate unexpected or expensive repair costs.

OTHER EXPENSES RELATED TO YOUR RV PURCHASE

Other expenses you need to consider as part of your RV purchase are sales taxes, registration, and insurance. These can vary widely depending on the state and county you live in at the time of purchase. It's important to mention this now because if you're planning on buying an RV to live in full-time, you may want to claim a new county or state as your residence first, to save money on your RV purchase and also down the road on registration and insurance. However, there are other factors to consider that may not make this a viable option. We'll talk about this more in Chapter 8 but wanted to at least mention it here, as this could change your RV purchase price by thousands of dollars.

Ultimately, we want you to be aware that while shopping for and buying an RV can be both exciting and fun, it can also be overwhelming. As you can see, there are several areas where you simply need to do your homework, crunch the numbers, and consider the risks as well as the rewards. Buying an RV can be a complex and costly exercise, but if you take your time, get educated, and make sound decisions that align with your budget and your goals, you will vastly increase your chances of success and a positive experience.

HOW DOES IT WORK?: UNDERSTANDING YOUR RV

What kinds of safety, repair, and maintenance skills do you need to have to live in an RV? These will all depend somewhat on the size and type of RV you choose, but most RVs have many systems in common. Some RVs are very basic, while others may be luxuriously appointed with more advanced technologies, bells, and whistles than many traditional homes.

Let's take you through the basics of understanding the major RV systems—water, electric, and other power sources—so you have an overview of how these important parts work.

MAKING SENSE OF YOUR RV SYSTEMS

Most RVers use water and electricity every waking hour, so don't think for a moment that you need to be roughing it when living in an RV! Most modern RVs can very easily accommodate both water and electricity when hooked up at a campsite and usually provide both even when parked in the middle of an open field or while driving! It's a pretty great feeling to know that you can be self-sufficient to a large degree.

First, let's take a look at the RV electrical system and explain the similarities and differences.

WHAT ELECTRICAL SYSTEMS DO RVS HAVE?

To power a traditional home in the US a utility company typically provides a consistent 110–120 volts of AC current. The amount of electricity you can use is virtually unlimited and available from any outlet in your home at all times.

While there are times when your RV will behave very similarly to your traditional home, the experience will vary a bit depending on your source of electricity and your RV's ability to accept that power. The wonderful additional option provided by your RV is that many of the basic functions will still operate during a power outage or when parked in the middle of nowhere. We've been in a campground that experienced a power and/or water outage and didn't even notice it for hours because we were using the systems onboard our RV!

When your RV is plugged into regular 110V AC power, electricity comes into your RV through a breaker panel to the 110V wall outlets and appliances. This external power will also be routed via a converter/charger to a battery (or group of batteries) that will store the power for future use. (Batteries can also be charged by the alternator on the engine of a motorhome or tow vehicle, or with solar power.)

Batteries provide power to the 12-volt electrical system within the RV. The 12V system will have its own fuse panel and will power things like the lights, water pump, fans, and monitoring electronics. Some more advanced RVs will also have an inverter that will allow the 12V power stored in the batteries to be converted back to 110V electricity to power outlets and small appliances.

YOUR RV WATER SYSTEMS

The water systems in your RV will function very much like those in a traditional home when you are hooked up at a campground or RV park, as long as it has what is called a "full hookup" (FHU) site. Full hookup means you have water, electric, and sewer connections at your campsite. Some campgrounds don't have sewer connections at the site, so you must dump your water and waste tanks at a central dump station. Other campgrounds might offer electricity only at the campsite, which means that you would need to fill your RV freshwater tank before getting situated in your site. The great news is that most RVs are well equipped to allow the water systems to function nearly the same as in a traditional home even when not hooked up directly to a water source. Most RVs have the ability to fill the freshwater tank by inserting a hose or pouring jugs of water into the tank. These freshwater tanks typically vary in size from 10

WHY WE LOVE RVING

"Our RV life gives us the freedom to go wherever we want to go and see whatever we want to see on our own time schedule."

Tom, 77, and Becky, 59

FULL-TIME RVERS SINCE APRIL 2015

WE FIRST STARTED CAMPING WITH A TENT THIRTEEN YEARS ago and our first night was a disaster, with a huge storm, freezing temps, and an air mattress that kept going down. After that terrible experience Becky never really wanted to go camping again—she preferred hotels! But the next year we bought a pop-up camper, which was much better. We actually changed RVs almost every year after that—mostly travel trailers—to accommodate our changing needs. We eventually came to really love being away in the camper and started considering living in an RV full-time. When we decided to go full-time, we were comfortable making a more significant investment and bought a new fifth wheel and a larger dually truck.

We knew we wanted to spend more time together, and with our age difference we didn't want to have to wait until Becky retired to travel and see more of the United States. We also didn't know how we would be able to afford to travel as much as we wanted with a house payment, property taxes, and utility bills going up every year. Realizing that this wasn't going to change, we decided to sell our house, pay everything off, and be debt-free, with a little left over for investments.

Our family thought it was a great idea—they know how we like to spend time together, so they were excited and very supportive. We normally like to spend summers in Pennsylvania, visiting our children, grandchildren, and great-grandchildren. But in the past couple of years we wanted to visit the Grand Canyon and Alaska, so we stayed on the West Coast. We try to spend six months in Pennsylvania and six months in the Southeast or Southwest—somewhere warm! As a nurse, Becky is able to find part-time work in Arizona and Florida in the winter.

We had planned on spending most of our time in campgrounds, not boondocking, and chose our RV accordingly, as we prefer residential appliances. We don't need a generator or solar installations, so we shop around for affordable RV parks and use our camping memberships to save money on where we stay. So far we have traveled to more than forty states and put more than 30,000 miles on our RV. It's allowed us to see places we never thought we would see before, and we love how affordably we can travel the country.

We think we are better off financially than if we had stayed in our house. If we had stayed, we would have both needed to still be working, but now we can get by with Becky working part-time six months of the year. It's all about re-prioritizing how you spend your money around what's more important to you—like experiences and travel. We used to move often in the early years, and in moving you tend to get rid of things . . . but we still had so much stuff! It can be hard getting rid of some things—like Tom's Corvettes; a 1966 and a 2008—but we know it's just stuff and when we leave this world it's not going with us anyway. After all, you never see a U-Haul behind a hearse!

to 100 gallons. RVs will also have a separate area where you can connect a hose to a fitting for a regular city water connection, which commonly offers the option of bypassing filling the freshwater tank.

The system will include a water pump that can pressurize the freshwater plumbing when not hooked up to city water. Similar to a traditional home, some water will flow to a water heater, and other water will flow directly to the faucets and toilets. When the wastewater is flushed down an RV toilet, it will flow into what is called the black tank. All other water that goes down the shower, kitchen, and bathroom sinks will flow into what is called the grey tank. The black and grey tanks have valves accessible outside the RV, and when they become full, you open the valves to drain the contents out of the tanks via a temporarily mounted sewer hose into an approved sewer drain or dump station.

One of the biggest differences between traditional home and RV water systems is that when water goes down the drain in your RV, that is not the last time you need to deal with it. The good news is that it is rarely the messy and horrific experience depicted in comedy movies like RV, starring Robin Williams. In fact, it is generally a very simple and sanitary process when handled properly—with gloves!

PROPANE SYSTEMS

The third significant system in RVs that differs from traditional homes is the use of propane fuel. Some homes in rural areas operate on propane, but most folks living in major metropolitan areas are used to having only natural gas, heating oils, or, in some cases, only electricity. Though some RVs can operate entirely on electricity, the majority of RVs will use propane for at least one appliance. Propane is commonly used for RV stovetops, furnaces, water heaters, and refrigerators. Residential refrigerators are becoming increasingly popular, but gas absorption RV fridges that operate on electricity and/or propane are historically more common.

STAYING SAFE WITH YOUR RV

Aside from the fact that your RV is a large moving vehicle, there are a lot of things to know to keep you, your traveling companions, and your home on wheels safe. Let's take a look at all the areas you need to be diligent about regarding RV safety.

WEIGHT SAFETY

There are many safety considerations to traveling and living in RVs, but perhaps the most overlooked safety element is weight, so let's address that one first.

It is estimated that more than 50 percent of RVs on the road today are overweight on at least one measurement. This could be their total weight or something more specific like hitch weight, axle weight, or tire weight ratings. Weight ratings are there for a reason, and if you travel while your RV is overweight, you could cause premature failure of components that could result in an accident. So, when you are looking at RVs, be sure to give special consideration to weight ratings and carry capacities in all areas of your setup, because the weight of all your clothes, gear, food, water, and anything else you travel with can add up fast.

TIRE SAFETY

Tire safety is largely related to the tires' weight capacities, but most RV and trailer tires are not rated for high speeds, which means you should not plan on traveling over 65 mph. It's very important to have the correctly rated tires for your RV and to keep your tires properly inflated at the correct PSI for your specific RV and tires.

Another often overlooked safety concern on RV tires is that RVs generally don't travel as many miles as regular passenger cars. This causes RV tires to "age out" before they wear out of tread. Keep track of the age of your RV tires and start considering replacement—or having them professionally inspected each year—if your tires are older than five years, regardless of remaining tread. If buying a used RV, be sure to check the date code on the tires, as this is far more important than any remaining tread.

PROPANE SAFETY

Propane and fire safety have additional considerations compared to traditional homes. The typical propane fridges used in RVs should be operated only when the RV is level, which means it is generally unsafe to leave them on while the vehicle is in motion, as you may be driving on steep grades or mountains. If they are operated off level for extended periods, they can fail and cause a fire. RV propane (not residential) refrigerators are one of the most common causes of RV fires, so it is very important that you stay mindful of keeping your RV and fridge level. It is especially unsafe

to enter a gas or propane fueling station with your RV fridge running since there is an open flame. The same goes for propane-powered water heaters and furnaces, so turn off your RV fridge, water heater, and furnace before refueling.

WATER SAFETY

Water safety in RVs relates to three key elements: pressure, leaks, and sanitation.

- **Pressure:** Some water sources, such as in a campground, will have water pressure as high as 120 psi, but RVs are generally designed for 60 psi. You can significantly reduce the risk of bursting lines in the RV causing leaks and water damage with a water pressure regulator.

- **Leaks:** Another source of leaks in RVs comes from the vehicle frequently being in motion, which can potentially loosen plumbing fixtures over time and make them subject to leaks. Keep an eye on them and tighten as needed.

- **Sanitation:** Sanitation is important because you are frequently changing the source of your water as you travel. Many RV parks use city water that is monitored regularly, but others might use well water or other less frequently monitored water sources. It is important to remember that not all water sources are created equally. For example, you should not use the water spigot at a dump station to add fresh water to your RV! It is recommended that you change your RV water filter regularly to keep your water clean.

ELECTRICAL SAFETY

Electrical safety is an important consideration because you are frequently changing the source of your electricity. Some RV parks have more stable electricity than others, and RV parks can see significant fluctuations in power compared to traditional homes. It's a good idea to have a surge protector, which ensures the energy is good quality when it reaches your RV. When arriving at a campsite, always be sure to turn off the breaker at the power pedestal before plugging your RV power cord into the post.

WEATHER SAFETY

Weather is another concern unique to RVs. Traditional homes are better equipped to withstand the expected weather in the area where they were built—whether that means better insulation from extreme temperatures, wind resistance, or even flood mitigation. RVers tend to follow the weather, heading south in the winter and north in the summer to avoid extreme temperatures. As an RVer, you should always pay close attention to the upcoming weather conditions as you travel so you can plan accordingly, be comfortable, and stay safe. Use the National Oceanic and Atmospheric Administration (NOAA) app or website (www.noaa.gov/weather), Google Alerts, and/or a weather radio to stay informed. If a hurricane is forecast, you probably should pack up your RV and leave for a safer area as soon as possible to avoid being at risk. If winds are high on a planned driving day, consider adjusting your schedule to avoid driving in windy conditions, which can be dangerous and make driving an RV much more difficult and fatiguing. Remember, you are the one in control of your schedule, so always keep an eye on the weather forecast, and if you have any concerns about what's ahead, move! If moving is not an option, seek out local storm shelters and have an emergency plan in place to minimize potential risk or damage.

DRIVING SAFETY

Driving an RV is different from driving a car, but as long as you are mindful of the differences, just about anyone can learn to safely drive or tow an RV. That said, we still think it's funny (and somewhat scary) that in some states you can drive up to an RV dealership in a compact car and drive off in a 45-foot-long diesel pusher motorhome weighing over 40,000 pounds. It is immediately evident that they are taller, longer, and wider than most passenger vehicles, but not everyone fully understands the impact of those increased dimensions. There's also the extra weight to consider.

1. **Height:** Many motorhomes and fifth wheel trailers are more than 12 feet tall. When you are driving your regular car, you probably don't think twice about driving into gas stations or under low bridges because you have

so much room above you, but in an RV those low bridges, gas stations, and low-hanging branches can cause severe damage to your vehicle.

2. **Width:** Most modern RVs are also wider than cars. Many are about 102 inches wide, which is about the same width as a semitruck and trailer. Highway lanes are generally 144 inches wide, so you will notice on highways that there is some room on both sides of large vehicles. Neighborhoods and small country roads are sometimes much narrower and are also more likely to have low-hanging trees, so you will need to pay more attention than you would in your car to avoid damage.

3. **Length:** The additional length of RVs brings a few important factors into play. In general, the length has little impact on wide-open highways—except when changing lanes, because you will need a much larger space to make a lane change, which means more planning. The larger impact of length shows up in corners, and in two ways.

   • You will need to make your turn later and sharper. If you take the corner like you would in a normal car, the rear axle or trailer will cut the corner, especially on a tight right-hand turn.

   • Be aware of tail-swing. You need to pay special attention to the length of RV behind the rear axle because in a sharp turn, the tail can swing out 1 foot for every 3 feet of length behind the rear axle. This means that the tail could swing out into the next lane in some cases, but it is generally more of a concern when maneuvering in tight spaces like gas stations or campsites. It is a good practice to not enter a parking lot or any other area unless you know in advance how you are going to make your exit! When it comes to driving an RV, you always need to be paying attention and thinking ahead.

4. **Weight:** With all the extra height, length, and width, it is easy to understand that your RV will also carry a bit of extra weight. This extra weight plays an important role in driving on hills, especially at higher elevations, and also on curvy roads. Even the most powerful RV will still struggle a bit compared to your car when climbing a steep hill, so you should plan on being in the slow lane on the highway on hills. The more important element of safety on hills is going downhill. All that additional weight can really push you down a hill, so you will need to use your gears, engine braking, and exhaust braking (if equipped) and maintain a slower speed to avoid overheating your regular brakes on your towing and towed vehicle.

With a little extra forethought, preparation, and practice you will be able to drive your RV almost as naturally as you drive your car or truck.

DEALING WITH RV MAINTENANCE, REPAIRS, AND BREAKDOWNS

Most RVers we meet spend a fraction of the time maintaining their RVs compared to the time they used to spend maintaining their traditional homes. It's a smaller space to take care of, there's no yard maintenance, and maintaining the home part of an RV is similar to maintaining a traditional home. There are exceptions to this, and we've met a few folks who have had more than their fair share of headaches, but remember, that can be the case with traditional homes too. Most of the regular maintenance, like cleaning and watching for leaks or wear and tear, is similar to that for a home. In RVs some screws and fixtures become loose more often because of all the movement of driving. Chassis, suspension, brake, and engine maintenance will vary depending on RV type and use but are generally less frequent than on a regular vehicle because most people don't travel as many miles in their RV as they do in their cars.

All that said, you need to know that repairs, breakdowns, and other unexpected challenges (and expenses) will happen with your RV from time to time. Some repairs are relatively simple, and if you are handy and brave enough to experiment, you can likely take care of some issues yourself—many don't usually require special tools. Often a quick search on *Google*, *YouTube*, or an RV owners' group forum will deliver a video, article, or other insight about doing the repair you are facing from someone who has been there before you. More advanced repairs will require a professional, but there are RV dealerships, service centers, and many mobile RV repair technicians all around the country. Sometimes you can get attention right away, and other times you may have to wait, so don't leave repairs until the last minute. If your RV is under factory warranty or you have an extended service contract, many of these repairs may be covered.

At the end of the day, no matter how well you take care of your RV, there's always a chance you'll be faced with an unexpected issue that leaves you immobilized, stranded on the side of the road, or requires expert assistance to get you on your way again, or safely relocated to a repair facility. It's a good idea to have emergency roadside assistance to protect you and provide peace of mind. We were on the road for two years before our first roadside assistance callout, and ended up using the service three times that year for different issues (tires, mechanical, and batteries).

You'll want a policy that provides suitable coverage for an RV, including unlimited towing—towing an RV can get very expensive! Most roadside assistance providers (like Coach-Net, Good Sam, and Progressive) are available 24/7 and have a large network of tow and service providers to assist you with mechanical or electrical breakdowns, battery jump starts, emergency fuel, flat tires, lockouts, and more. Some providers like Coach-Net also offer technical and

WHY WE LOVE RVING

Nik, 31, and Allison, 30

STARTED RVING FULL-TIME IN MAY 2016 AND STOPPED IN OCTOBER 2017

Website: http://therecklesschoice.com

Instagram: @therecklesschoice

"We loved the RV lifestyle because we love camping and exploring, and living full-time in an RV allowed us to do both of those things all the time."

IN 2012, WHEN NIK GOT A JOB THAT ENABLED HIM TO WORK remotely from anywhere in the world, we made a list that was part bucket list, part remote work adventures. It included things like "RV around the country," "Take a round-the-world flight," "Help my parents start a bike tour business," and more. We kept the list on the fridge for a year, and as time went on, full-time RVing stood out as the option for us.

Once we'd decided on RVing, we still had a lot of decisions to make. We eventually wanted kids, and Nik wanted to be a stay-at-home dad when that happened. Given that Nik was also the primary earner, we needed to manage our spending and plan on a ton of savings before we had kids. Financial advisers often recommend that you save 15 percent of your income for retirement, but we usually save more than 50 percent. We are very intentional about how we spend our money to make sure we are getting as much happiness as possible from our spending.

That mindset spilled over into planning for RVing. Luckily, we realized that RVing doesn't need to be expensive, and even if Allison couldn't work full-time while we were on the road, we'd still end up ahead financially. We knew that we wanted to camp for free on public lands, not only because it was free but also because we got much more enjoyment from the solitude and views offered by boondocking compared to feeling like sardines in campgrounds. To access those free sites we knew we'd need a rig that was small enough to get off the paved roads. We didn't want to listen to a generator or pay for the fuel to run it, so that meant we needed solar panels. Most important-ly, we chose to buy a used RV and renovate it rather than buying new. We found a 1989 motorhome that we loved for $6,500 and spent an-other $5,000 renovating it. Compared to the similarly sized $100,000 new RVs we looked at, we saved a lot of years of stay-at-home-dad time without sacrificing much in the way of enjoyment.

While we were full-timing, we traveled 10,000 miles through ten states and two Canadian provinces, visited eighteen national parks and countless national forests and monuments, and had a ball doing it! Eventually, we realized we desired a closer sense of community and friends whom we could see over and over again every week; plus, Allison wanted to get back to her teaching career. To top it off, we were considering adoption as a way to expand our family, a pro-cess that isn't really feasible for full-time RVers. So Allison found a great job back in Colorado near some of our friends, and we decided to move back into a house. We'll definitely hit the road again during school breaks, but for the moment building relationships with our friends and expanding our family are our top priorities.

operational assistance over the phone. You may be able to get (or already have) roadside assistance through your RV manufacturer, auto insurer, or even within your extended service contract. Just be sure to check the policy details to ensure you have adequate coverage for your needs.

You'll also want to carry some roadside emergency safety items like traffic cones, LED beacons, and a reflective vest to keep you safe on the side of the road. Get our Roadside Safety Gear and Checklist at our website https://rvlove.com/book-bonus-content.

Keep in mind that while RV breakdowns and repairs happen to most of us at some point, it's easier to get through it by staying calm, focusing on solutions, and keeping your sense of humor. Eventually, with experience and a few repairs behind you, you'll start viewing issues as an opportunity for learning and part of the adventure. They usually make great campfire stories too!

PART 2

EMOTIONAL CONSIDERATIONS

Making the decision to embrace the RV lifestyle involves many emotional considerations you may not have thought about. As you get ready to hit the road, it's natural to go through a range of feelings—from the excitement of travel and adventures to the sadness of leaving your home, community, and support network behind. You may also feel fear about leaving behind the familiar and have mixed feelings about stepping into unknown territory. As an RVer, you'll be constantly changing your environment, trying to stay connected with people back at home, and perhaps navigating the art of small-space living with other people. You'll find yourself needing to create new routines and habits and explore ways to take care of your health as you travel—all while constantly learning new things and trying to make sense of all the ins and outs of your RV!

But don't let the emotional considerations overwhelm you. It takes time to adjust to the full-time RV lifestyle, and the experience will be different for everyone, so take a deep breath and know we've got your back! Here in Part 2 we'll cover the most important things you'll need to help you prepare for your transition to the RV life and make your journey as smooth as possible.

and/or nature. Shared experiences deepen a personal connection. Think of the people you worked, studied, or played sports with in the past. Those experiences created a bond and connection that you don't have with others you meet. Perhaps you and your partner share a hobby, an interest, or a "why" for living the lifestyle that you will want to do on your travels to increase positive experiences together. Do you have a bucket list of things you want to experience while you can? Perhaps you're a food lover wanting to go on a culinary journey. Do you want to take your kids to every national park or state capital? Maybe you are a fan of lighthouses or baseball stadiums and want to visit them all. How do you want to grow as a person, couple, or family through this? Considering these questions can help you focus on what is driving your decision to do this instead of focusing on the inevitable challenges.

Leaving behind some of the stresses of your old life, being out in nature, hiking, and exploring national parks make it easier to relax, feel grounded, and keep perspective.

COMMUNICATE AND BE PATIENT

If emotions come up, it can be helpful to talk about what you're going through with your partner, a friend, or a family member who is supportive of your decision. You may be excited about your plans and yet be completely sidelined by unexpected feelings of sadness too. Sit down with your partner (and kids, if you're traveling as a family) and have an open, honest conversation about the possibility that all kinds of feelings may come up as you transition to RV life. You may be grieving what you've left behind, and this takes time to process. Here are some tips for communicating effectively about your change:

- Give each other permission to experience whatever you're feeling and share it, without judgment.
- Plan on giving each other additional support, grace, and patience, especially during the first several months.
- Try to do small but loving things to show your partner you care.
- Discuss what you can do to create an environment that will support harmonious living for everyone.
- Talk about your concerns but also what excites you and what you're looking forward to, to keep the balance.

One of the great advantages of living in the smaller space of an RV is that there is no room for small issues to silently grow into big problems, which means you are forced to address them sooner. Because you aren't spending time in different rooms of a bigger house, living in the smaller space makes you much more keenly aware of each other's emotions, which helps with understanding and communication. We have met many couples with deep, loving connections on the road. We've met couples on the brink of divorce who healed their marriage after living in an RV. And we've met couples who had been married for decades before discovering that life on the road together wasn't what they wanted and ended up deciding to go their separate ways. RV life isn't the miracle cure for problems, but it can help shine a light on what's really going on in a relationship as well as ways to deal with it. There is a lot to learn in transitioning to this new lifestyle, so be patient with each other.

TRAVELING WITH KIDS

Perhaps one of the first considerations when you think about RVing with kids is where they are going to sleep without affecting the livability of your RV. A bunkhouse, over-cab bed, pull-out sofa, or dinette can be a good option, or even an inflatable mattress for short-term stays. There are some RVs—motorhomes and fifth wheels—with two bedrooms, and we've seen RVers convert the garage of their toy hauler into a second bedroom. Some also choose RVs with one and a half bathrooms.

MANAGING ALL THE PERSONALITIES

There are thousands of families traveling full-time in an RV with anywhere from one to a dozen (or more) kids of all ages, including some with special needs. Of course, the more people traveling in your RV, the more energy, bodies, and personalities you'll have to deal with 24/7. On one hand, you all know each other well, so you probably know what to expect. But that also means there is literally no space for problems to grow, so you can't sweep issues under the rug. You'll need to work together as a family to find solutions that work for everyone. Here are some examples of how full-time RVing families navigate the inevitable challenges:

- Set up a tent to give kids a space to make a mess.
- To break a bad mood or attitude do a bath/shower time to "wash off the angries," followed by a hug.
- If they wake early, have a banana and PBS Kids shows ready to occupy them until you're ready.

- A good walk in the rain or wind can be very cleansing for everyone.
- Have a weekly campfire powwow with no electronics, and give everyone a chance to air grievances, listen to each other, and come up with ideas for future plans and things to do, and finish with a sweet treat, like s'mores.

Many families we've met have become much closer through traveling together in an RV by sharing experiences and being active witnesses as they learn, grow, and try new things all day, every day.

THE NOISE FACTOR

With kids, there's going to be more noise (laughing, talking, yelling), more stuff, and more mess, and with RVs not being as big or well insulated as houses, you'll need to be mindful of this in RV parks and campgrounds where you're situated close to other RVers. Camping in national and state parks, family-focused campgrounds, and on free public lands (BLM land) can sometimes be more family-friendly because they provide more space for kids to get outside and play while providing opportunities to explore nature, increasing their adventurous spirit and confidence.

ROADSCHOOLING

School-age children usually learn via online schools or by parents homeschooling (roadschooling) them from the RV, as well as in libraries, national parks, and the biggest classroom there is—the real world! Homeschooling is legal throughout the United States, but the laws can vary from state to state, so visit https://hslda.org/laws to check the rules for the state you're from or that you plan to select as your domicile.

FINDING TIME ALONE AS PARENTS

Traveling with kids can also limit private time for parents. Finding other families to travel or spend time with is a great way to not only form friendships but also share parental supervision and give each couple some kid-free together time. Organizations like FulltimeFamilies.com (with more than 20,000 members) offer a fantastic support network for RVers with kids. They share advice and resources and host regular rallies around the country. This can be a great way for parents and kids to connect, create new friendships, get support, and learn from each other.

TRAVELING WITH PETS

Pets are a big part of the RV lifestyle, with dogs and cats being the most common. The most unusual RVing pets we've seen and heard of are owls, a bearded dragon, and a full-sized pig! Yes, almost anything goes when it comes to RVing, but do be aware that some RV parks and campgrounds may have restrictions around what pets you travel with and how many. We've seen some RV parks that limit RVers to two dogs or don't allow certain breeds (e.g., Dobermans, German shepherds, pit bulls, Rottweilers). Many RV parks have a dog run or dog park where you can take your furry friends out to play, but be aware that national parks generally have very few trails that allow pets. You can find useful tips and information at PetFriendlyTravel.com.

GETTING YOUR PET USED TO THE RV

Of course, your pets are part of your family and may also be affected by the changes going on all around them. When moving out of a familiar, comfortable home with all of their favorite smells and spots, it can take time for them to adjust to their new RV environment. Consider what space will be allocated to your pets in the RV, and perhaps modify your space to suit their needs. It can be a good idea to spend some time relaxing or working in your RV with your pet before fully moving in to help them get used to it before you head off.

VET CONSIDERATIONS

You'll want to be sure that your pets have had vet appointments before you leave and are up to date with their shots. Take copies of your vet records and vaccine certificates as well as any necessary medications with you. We recommend joining a national pet healthcare chain like Banfield Pet Hospital, which keeps a centralized record of your pet's health history in their computer system no matter where you travel. They also offer a pet care plan, which

you may want to consider, as your pets will be exposed to more things and a range of environments as you travel. National chain pet stores also offer a range of supplies and services, like grooming, training, doggie daycare, pet sitting, dog walking, and pet boarding. There are even apps like Rover and Wag if you need a pet walker, sitter, or drop-in visits for pets left alone in the RV for a period of time.

OTHER TIPS

Here are some other things to think about regarding your pet:

- **Temperature:** Be mindful of keeping your RV at a comfortable temperature for your pets, especially if you'll be leaving them unattended on hot days. Many RVers install a system that starts an onboard generator automatically if there's a power failure at a campground, ensuring that the inside temperature doesn't get too high.

- **Special food or medications:** If your pet needs medication or a special brand of food, stock up before you leave, as it's not always easy to find these things as you travel.

- **Connecting with other pet owners online:** There are several dog-friendly social media groups available on *Facebook* and RVillage.com where you can do a search for, connect with, and even meet other pet owners along your travels. Sites like http://tailsfromtheroad.com and *Facebook* groups like Camping and RVing with Pets and RVing with Dogs on *Facebook* are good options.

ALIGN ON YOUR TRAVEL STYLE AND PACE AHEAD OF TIME

Similar to getting on the same page with your big vision for your RV life and travel itinerary, you will also want to agree with your RV companion on a travel style and pace. You might not fully know what your travel pace will be until you settle into your life on the road, but it's important to discuss your vision before you head out. For example, your vision might be to stay on paved, level sites at high-end RV parks, while your partner wants to stay in more rustic or remote off-grid locations that may offer peace and scenery but also require you to heavily conserve power and water. Your vision might be to fully immerse yourself in each area and only change locations every month or two, while your travel partner might prefer to move at a faster pace, staying only a few nights in each location.

MANAGING THE LOGISTICS OF RV LIVING

Just like in regular home living, the people in your RV will relax, make messes, and do chores. The key to keeping everyone happy and life running smoothly in your moving home is to think about these things ahead of time so you can make a plan that works for everyone.

WHAT DOES DOWNTIME LOOK LIKE FOR EACH PERSON?

Know yourself and everyone traveling with you! You might be an introvert and need time alone to recharge. Your partner might be an extrovert who needs high levels of socialization for optimal happiness. Knowing your own needs as well as the needs of your partner and/or kids might help you decide whether you plan to stay in RV parks that offer higher levels of interaction with others or choose to boondock without hookups in your RV out in the middle of nowhere. You can almost always find downtime, but if you are camping out in the middle of miles of open land and one of you has high social needs, you'll need to find a way to accommodate those needs, perhaps through social media or phone calls. Either way, you'll both need to be flexible and go with the flow as much as possible.

SPEND SOME TIME APART

Of course, one of the best parts of full-time or extended RV travel is that most RVers tend to follow the weather and are therefore almost always in environments that allow them to spend more time outside of the RV. This is a great opportunity for you and your travel companions to get outside for a bit of separation when needed, as even the closest couples will benefit from downtime or a little time apart. You can go for a walk or a bike ride, call a friend, go to the laundry or grocery store, or take your laptop down to the campground lodge or local coffee shop. If you travel

Your plans may change once you hit the road, but if you don't discuss your preferred style and pace of travel early on and get on the same page, it could be a recipe for trouble. Keep the lines of communication open, consider each person's needs, and give yourselves time to find the groove that works best for you both. Most RVers tend to start traveling at a fast pace because we're so excited about our adventures and want to see as much as we can, but most of us learn soon enough to slow down, to enjoy the journey and avoid burning out.

in a motorhome with a separate towed vehicle, you may even occasionally choose to drive separately on travel days, especially if you find driving relaxing, as we both do.

INVEST IN BIG HEADPHONES!

When it comes to living in a small space, even things like the TV, music, or loud phone calls can become a source of annoyance, as you can't escape to different parts of the house like you used to. In an RV you can hear just about everything! We recommend a good set of the larger, overear headphones as an excellent way of creating your own space and downtime. When you each have your own set of headphones, you can watch TV or videos, listen to music, make a phone call, or simply enjoy silence without affecting anyone else in the RV. The overear headphones are a good choice for a few reasons:

1. They are more comfortable to wear, especially for long periods of time.
2. They are better for minimizing noise so you can relax or concentrate, without being bothered by other noises or distractions.
3. They also serve as a visual signal to others that you want some downtime or are focused on something else.

Putting on your own set of quality headphones is like stepping into your own room or personal zone and is well worth the investment in your RV life and relationship.

TEAMWORK WITH JOBS AND TASKS

Many people we meet on the road tend to be compatible and consider themselves a team, which helps with harmonious living in their RV. A big part of being a team is dividing and conquering the jobs and tasks that come with RV living so it

feels fair and equitable and you are each doing the jobs you prefer. There are also many new and different tasks that you might not have had in your previous lifestyle. Deciding who handles which jobs establishes responsibility and also ensures that one person is not carrying the entire load, which helps build the team feeling. It also helps you finish tasks sooner, allowing for more time to enjoy the best parts of the lifestyle.

Write down a list of all the jobs—inside and outside your RV—and let each person pick which things they prefer doing so that you both have jobs you like or are best suited for. One person's preferred tasks might be completely different from the other's, which will allow for a very easy split of tasks. If you both dislike certain tasks, divide them up or take turns.

"Give yourself a good six months on the road to adjust. It's a big change and it will be hard at times. RV life isn't all sunshine and rainbows; you have to dump your poop tank too!"

—Caitlin Morton, full-time RVer

And be sure to create a good system for navigating and parking the RV! While it is possible to navigate and park the RV yourself, it is safer and generally easier when you have a helper. When it comes to parking your RV, be sure to agree on hand signals and communication ahead of time—especially the signal to stop. Try practicing your parking teamwork in an empty parking lot with safety cones before trying it in a campground with trees and an audience. Cell phones and/or walkie-talkie two-way radios are also good, as they prevent the need for shouting commands that can quickly raise tension. When couples have a clear understanding of who does what in an RV, it helps create a sense of purpose and responsibility, reduces miscommunication, avoids important things being missed or forgotten, and helps prevent resentment building if one feels like they are doing more than the other.

AVOIDING CLUTTER IN A SMALL SPACE

Any time you live with others there's usually one person with a higher tolerance for clutter—leaving things outside of their assigned space—than the other. When you have a large home, you and your partner might have your own rooms or spaces for your stuff (e.g., office or craft room) and more ways for those differences to live in harmony. However, an RV is a much smaller space with fewer rooms, and generally almost all of the RV is shared space. So it's more important to be aligned and pay attention to clutter in your RV, especially as things generally need to be put away to safely travel. These three tips will save you a lot of clutter and frustration:

1. Give everything a home and put things away when not in use.

2. Don't buy stuff as you travel; take photos instead of buying souvenirs.

3. Clean out every so often—try to adopt a "one thing in, one thing out" mentality so you don't collect too much.

If you are the kind of person who leaves things out instead of storing them neatly inside cupboards, you will not only need more time to pack down and set up your RV on travel days, but it could also lead to more tension, especially if the tidy partner has to pack the other's things every time you move. Living in an RV means you need a heightened awareness and commitment to being more considerate and mindful of your traveling companion's needs, to avoid unnecessary frustration and conflict.

"Everything must have a home and be put back in place every time it is used. Seek out items that stack, nest, or fold. You will master your organization skills for sure."

—Jennifer Braga, full-time RVer

MAKING YOUR RV FEEL LIKE HOME

It's rare to find an RV that is just so perfect that you won't want or need to make any changes for it to suit your full-time RV life. Things that may be easy to deal with on weekends or vacations are often not so desirable when living in your RV full-time. Fortunately, it's easy enough to make your RV feel like your home, with some decorating, upgrades, modifications, and personal touches.

Of course, some RVs might be styled beautifully from day one and perfectly fit your individual tastes. Simply bringing your clothes and kitchenware onboard may be all it takes for you to settle in. Other RVs might require a complete makeover before they will meet your needs or feel like home. Many RVs have many cabinets for storage, which can reduce the wall space available for hanging pictures or artwork, so you may need to get creative with placement of photos or artwork to personalize your RV, or use a digital photo frame. Most RV interiors tend to have a lot of browns, beiges, and other earthy tones, but if that's not your style, don't be afraid to lighten and brighten up your RV's interior and decorate it to reflect your personality.

Changing the interior styling can affect resale, especially on newer RVs, but the most important thing is that you feel at home, especially if you plan on living in it for a long time! So if that means painting the walls, updating window coverings, converting a bunkhouse into an office (as we did), or replacing furniture with something that better suits you, do it! We have seen some amazing makeovers and upgrades to RVs that can have you wondering if you are even inside an RV at all.

RV TERMS TO KNOW

bunkhouse: A separate room or dedicated area in an RV with built-in bunk beds for kids (usually two bunks; sometimes more). This can also be referred to as a bunk room.

slide topper: A fabric or vinyl cover attached to the side of an RV and covering the top of the slideout room to protect it from weather, debris, etc.

The first thing we did to our two-year-old RV was convert the bunkhouse into a dedicated office for Marc to work from. This made our RV perfect for our needs for almost four years until we felt ready for a change. In 2018 we bought a much older, much less expensive motorhome that was high quality but in need of a makeover, so we made a number of modifications and upgrades to reflect our style and evolving needs. We upgraded and modernized it to rival some of the newer ones we had been looking at, for a fraction of the cost, and really made it our own. You can see what we did at our *RVLove* website, *YouTube* channel (www.youtube.com/rvlove), and social media pages. You can also check out other RVers' social media pages for inspiration and find many great ideas on *Pinterest, Instagram,* and *Facebook.*

When it comes to RV upgrades, the sky's the limit. You could install a solar power system (as we did) to fully enable your off-grid lifestyle, customize storage solutions to accommodate specialized hobby gear, or even create a pet ramp and doggie door for your furry friends. The opportunities are truly endless and limited only by your creativity and imagination. Over the years we've seen everything—from vintage travel trailers and Airstream renovations to fifth wheel makeovers, Class A modifications, and even bus conversions!

COMMON RV UPGRADES AND MODIFICATIONS

- ☐ Converting a bunkhouse into an office, extra-large closet, or pet kennel area
- ☐ Converting a toy hauler garage into a bedroom or office
- ☐ Creating spaces for work or schooling
- ☐ Painting or wallpapering walls
- ☐ Updating décor, such as window valances and furniture upholstery
- ☐ Changing the bed size from queen to king and vice versa
- ☐ Modifying for the needs of owners with a disability or specialized physical need
- ☐ Creating dedicated pet areas and ramps
- ☐ Replacing carpet with vinyl, tile, wood, or even heated flooring
- ☐ Recovering or replacing furniture
- ☐ Replacing fluorescent or halogen lighting with LED lighting and new light fixtures
- ☐ Replacing window awnings and adding slide toppers
- ☐ Converting a second bathroom into an additional storage area or closet
- ☐ Adding an outside TV or portable cooler
- ☐ Replacing RV fridges with residential refrigerators
- ☐ Upgrading a propane range top to an induction cooking plate
- ☐ Removing an RV oven to install a dishwasher
- ☐ Adding a washer/dryer (space and plumbing permitting)
- ☐ Upgrading the kitchen with new countertops and sinks
- ☐ Upgrading the kitchen and bathroom faucets with residential-style fixtures
- ☐ Upgrading to a lithium battery bank
- ☐ Full solar installations, with solar panels and inverter
- ☐ Installing a composting toilet to extend off-grid living
- ☐ Creating a "man cave" in the RV basement/storage area (or garage in some models) for tools
- ☐ Repainting the exterior or doing a full (or partial) vinyl body wrap for a fresh new look

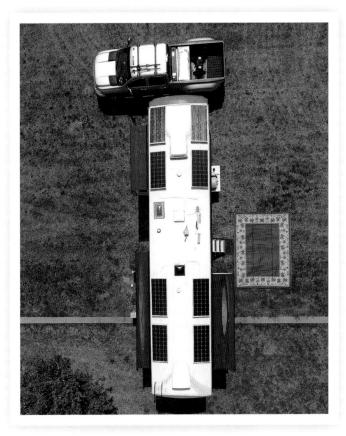

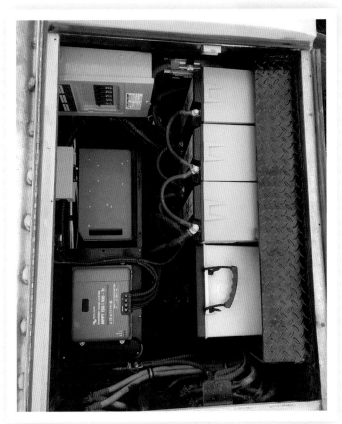

Ultimately, the more homey your RV feels and the better designed it is for your unique needs, the longer you will feel comfortable living in it. This in turn may help reduce the frequency of changing RVs, which can reduce the financial impact of trade-ins, offsetting depreciation to some degree. Just remember that RVs are not like houses in that they rarely appreciate and mostly depreciate. So you probably don't want to overinvest in renovations, as that's money you're unlikely to get back when you sell your RV, but it will make your living environment much more enjoyable. And always keep RV weight in mind to ensure that you don't exceed the safe, legal weight with modifications and upgrades—it's always a delicate balance.

WHY WE LOVE RVING

"The RV lifestyle is a remarkable freedom from life's leashes—homeownership, jobs that control us, clutter and chaos, and a 'keeping up with the Joneses' mentality. This nomadic lifestyle allows us to be ourselves while also traveling to places we've never seen."

Dan, SS, and Lisa, SS

FULL-TIME RVERS SINCE APRIL 2014

Website: http://alwaysonliberty.com
Instagram: @alwaysonliberty
Facebook: Always on Liberty
Pinterest: Always on Liberty

WE'VE BEEN NOMADS MOST OF OUR LIVES DUE TO MILITARY service. Once Dan retired from the Coast Guard, we felt out of sorts. We were accustomed to moving often. Our big Kentucky home was our pride and joy, yet it just wasn't where our restless souls belonged.

We're both adventurous and had ridden motorcycles on cross-country adventures, but we always felt that bondage of having to return to the stresses of jobs and the responsibilities and work that come with home ownership. We yearned to see what was on the other side of that mountain, up the river, and down in the canyons. We're not "sideline" people—we had a strong sense of yearning to GO and DO.

So we bought a new fifth wheel and dually truck, hit the road with our two cats, and felt this exhilaration we'd never felt before—facing the unknown along with the excitement of new places and meeting great people along the way. We mostly enjoy boondocking, living off the grid, and finding cool "off-the-map" places to park and step outside.

Now that we've grown to love our 360-square-foot home on wheels and plan to be doing this indefinitely, we decided to really personalize our RV to make it our "home." We wanted to bring in more color and fun motifs to create a relaxing, breezy Key West cottage feel, instead of the traditional RV browns and beiges. Lisa took on the job of stylist, while Dan agreed to do the labor.

The inspiration for our color palette came from a picnic plate we found—it had a bold pattern and bright colors that we fell in love with. We sourced fabric and paint to match, picked a lighter wood-look vinyl floor tile, and created a style board that showed us the "vision."

We boldly stepped out of the norm to paint the ceilings white to blend with the ceiling vents for a more professional, clean look and painted the walls margarita green, poppy, and aqua. We installed new flooring, covered the valances, and created a unique kitchen galley backsplash. We removed a sofa and put in a desk to create an awesome new workspace that faces whatever view is outside our huge back window. We added finishing touch-es by snapping up sale items such as creative and colorful drawer pulls and quirky knobs for the cupboards, while beachy handcrafted artwork and repurposed photo frames completed the look.

This "home" personalization has really emphasized our happy-go-lucky, spontaneous personalities. Each morning, as we walk down into the galley and living area, we are met with bright sunshine and color to start our day. We love looking out of our big back window to be inspired by the mountains, lakes, trees, sunrises, and sunsets. Our two cats each have their own comfortable matching cat beds on either side of the workspace table/desk so they can watch the birds and wildlife or nap.

Our RV makeover accomplished everything we had envisioned and more! Everyone who visits our home on wheels seems instantly inspired to step out of their own comfort zone to do the same, saying, "We can do this to ours too!"

CHAPTER 5

STAYING CONNECTED

Keeping In Touch with People On and Off the Road

"A journey is best measured in friends rather than miles."

—Tim Cahill, American travel writer

You may be leaving behind your family, friends, and community, but there's a whole other world of friendships out there just waiting be discovered! We humans are meant to connect with one another, so it's only natural to be concerned about feeling lonely on the road. The great news is that you get to choose how private or social to be and what kinds of people to spend your time with, plus when, where, and how often.

Thanks to technology, it's easy to stay in touch with those you love back at home while also finding and making new friends on the road. As an RVer, you'll meet many people along your travels, build a new community of like minds, and discover groups and events that interest you. It may take a little time, a little patience, and a willingness to put yourself out there, but you will find your tribe. Let's explore some of the ways you can do that.

STAYING IN TOUCH WITH FAMILY AND FRIENDS BACK HOME

If one of your biggest fears about living the full-time RV life is the prospect of leaving behind your family, friends, and community, don't worry—you're not alone! This is a common concern for many considering the RV lifestyle. Typically you will also be leaving your support network, whether that's friends, family, work colleagues, neighbors, or even favorite local businesses you've supported over the years.

Although it can be exciting to think about all the new people you will meet, as well as the idea of visiting family and friends around the country, it can still be hard to consider what might happen to your established relationships in the area you depart from. You—or those who remain—might feel a sense of separation or even abandonment once you leave. This can be especially challenging for some parents and grandparents leaving their children and grandchildren. Following are some suggestions for how you can ease the transition and continue to maintain strong and healthy relationships with those who matter most.

STAY LOCAL FOR A WHILE

You can live in your RV for a few weeks or even a few months in the general area to give you a chance to familiarize yourself with a different kind of home without needing to be in a different area of the country. Invite family and friends over to visit to help them feel like they're part of your RV life.

PLAN ON REGULAR RETURN VISITS

Even while exploring the country you can plan on returning to your former hometown as often as you like, and this does not always have to mean traveling back with your RV. Plan to return every so often to visit family, friends, or doctors as needed. This may be easy if you are traveling slowly or staying in the same general area of the country, but if you're from Maine and find yourself in California, it won't always make sense to drive your RV back. And returning home for the holidays if you're from a cold or snowy place won't be as comfortable or safe in an RV, so you may want to fly into town for some of your visits.

INVITE THEM TO VISIT YOU

Whether you invite people to come and stay in your RV or in a cabin, a local hotel, or their own rented RV, your RV lifestyle also provides a great opportunity to inspire family and friends to plan a vacation and visit you anywhere in the country! Keep in mind that RVs are small spaces, and anything more than a weekend may feel like a long time if you're hosting guests in your home on wheels. If we have guests wanting to visit for more than a couple of nights, we'll typically suggest a cabin or nearby hotel; that way, we can have our own space, they can have theirs, and we can still enjoy time together.

MAKE VIDEO CALLS

Of course, one of the best ways to stay connected with people is through technology. While social media, email, and phone calls are great, video calls—through FaceTime, Skype, *Facebook*, or Google Hangouts—can be even better, as it's almost like catching up in person. Set up a computer, tablet, or smartphone on the dining table for coffee or happy-hour dates so you can catch up face-to-face over a good long chat. You can even share your current view by turning the camera around and showing it to them in real time. You'll need a strong cellular signal and plenty of data on your phone/Internet plan for video calls—we'll cover that topic in Chapter 7.

USE SOCIAL MEDIA

There are many ways you can help make people feel they are still connected with your life as you travel. You can do this through regular social media updates, but you may also want to consider setting up a dedicated website, blog, *Facebook* page, *Instagram* feed, or *YouTube* channel for sharing your RV travels. You can make these public or private, granting access to only a select group of people. This way, only the people who are truly interested in that side of your life can follow your journey.

Many people we know, families especially, want to share their adventures with family and friends and keep a progressive online "diary" with photos and updates on where they went and what they saw, did, and learned. If you want to keep things simple with the least amount of time and effort, consider creating a basic *Facebook* page specific to your RV life and adventures and invite your family and friends to like or follow it. It doesn't require any learning of new technology and will free up your time for the things that matter more, like being in the moment and enjoying your experiences, instead of being focused on how to capture and share them.

KEEP YOUR CLOSEST FAMILY MEMBERS IN THE LOOP

For your nearest and dearest it may be important for you to maintain a sense of continuity and even reach out more often than usual as you transition to your RV life. Marc is close to his mom and she was sad about us leaving, so he increased the frequency of his calls to her, and he also calls or texts to let her know every time we get settled into a new campground. That way, she always has peace of mind knowing where we are, feels like she's part of our everyday life, and also gets to share our latest news or travels with the rest of the family, keeping everyone in the loop.

DON'T OVERSHARE

While some people will love living vicariously through you and feel like they are part of your travels, not everyone will want to see or hear all about the amazing experiences you're having in your new, adventurous life. It may be challenging for others and even cause some envy, as they may compare your experience to their more "normal" and less exciting life or think you are boasting. Be sensitive when it comes to sharing (or oversharing) your experiences, and always ask others about what's going on in their lives when you catch up.

UNDERSTAND THAT SOME RELATIONSHIPS WILL CHANGE

Despite your efforts to stay connected, you must still be prepared for the reality that some of your relationships will change. Your deepest and most connected relationships will likely remain, but your more casual relationships may eventually fall away, as some people only put effort into relationships that are geographically convenient. Over time you may find that you have less in common with many people back home than you do with the people you meet out on the road. While it can be sad seeing or feeling relationships change or fade away, keep perspective on what you are gaining in your life, instead of focusing on any perceived losses. The relationships that really matter to you will remain intact, especially if you plan to return to the area often or are planning to RV only for a limited time.

MAKE PLANS FOR SPECIAL EVENTS AND HOLIDAYS

It won't be possible for you to get back home for every birthday party, holiday, or special event. But you may want to make plans to return for the most important ones, like weddings, graduations, and milestone birthdays or anniversaries. We know some RVers who go home for major holidays and some who don't—it's a personal choice.

We try to alternate and return to Colorado every other year to see family for the holidays. When we can't be there, we find creative ways to participate. For example, if the family is getting together for Thanksgiving dinner, we often make a FaceTime call after their meal, when we know they are relaxing in the living room. They pass around the iPad for an hour or two, which gives us a chance to visit with everyone—and we feel like we are actually there!

MAKE THE MOST OF YOUR TIME TOGETHER

When you sit back and take an honest look at your traditional life, like many, you may realize that while you live in the same town, some people's lives are so busy that you may not get to see each other as often as you would like anyway. When you're back for visits less often, you may find that those who really want to see you will make a more significant effort to meet up and be more present in your time together. Since hitting the road we have definitely found that while there's less time spent with loved ones, it's now more focused quality time. We really appreciate the time we do get to spend together, instead of taking it for granted.

PUT IN A LITTLE EXTRA EFFORT

Keep in mind that because you are the one who made the decision to leave, you will also probably be the one who needs to put a little extra effort into your relationships after you've left. You'll want to make sure that those closest to you still feel loved and know you haven't forgotten about them while you're off on your RV adventures. Soon enough they will get used to it, too, and you may even find that your relationships improve as a result.

WHY WE LOVE RVING

Nathan, 37, Marissa, 32, and Hensley, 4

FULL-TIME RVERS SINCE MAY 2015

Website: https://lessjunkmorejourney.com

YouTube: Less Junk, More Journey

Instagram: @lessjunkmorejourney

Facebook: Less Junk, More Journey

"Let's sell our house and move into a camper!" Words I never thought I would hear my husband say, much less words I would agree to. Surprisingly, here we are living in our Airstream and having the adventure of a lifetime.

WE STRUGGLED WITH INFERTILITY AND, AFTER MUCH PRAYER and many tears, were blessed with an amazing daughter, changing our lives forever. Her arrival sparked an interest in us as parents to have a life of "Less Junk, More Journey." Life was good, but we knew there was more to life than the daily grind and keeping up with the Joneses. We wanted a life of adventure and memories.

We decided to sell our house and move into an RV to travel the country and live a simpler life of freedom and family time. It was a crazy and scary transition moving from a house to a camper with a little one, but after three years of living full-time in an RV, we wouldn't have it any other way. We decided we would rather regret a decision we made than regret one we did not make out of fear.

When we began our travels, we thought it would be about family time and adventure. One of the best surprises of full-time travel has been community. We've met amazing people along the way whom we otherwise would never have crossed paths with—people from all walks of life who have taught us different ways to view the world.

Our first year on the road was lonely. We thought meeting people would be easy but then realized we had to be intentional about it. We attended our first Fulltime Families Rally and were immediately hooked. Community was what was missing when we first left, but we have since made friendships that will last a lifetime. We now

make rallies and events part of our travels to allow for a greater sense of community.

We are both introverts, so reaching out to others was challenging for us, as was our decision to film our lives and put it on *YouTube*. We had to step out of our box but have grown as people from that. Through our *YouTube* channel, Less Junk, More Journey, we have connected more easily with people on the road, opening the door to meet other like-minded people.

While we wanted this journey to bond our family, we didn't want to sacrifice our relationships with friends and extended family. We found a sweet spot with an amount of time we like to explore the country and then return to visit our loved ones at our "home base" in Tennessee. We still go home for the holidays and spend one or two months there in the spring or summer. It's a good balance of travel and time with family.

We also have family members fly out to join our adventures. Having Marissa's mom stay with us at the Grand Canyon was a memory of a lifetime. Her sisters have flown out to join us, and friends have taken road trips to meet us for beach camping. Sharing our journey with family and friends has been an incredible way to make memories together and keep our relationships vibrant.

FINDING YOUR TRIBE ON THE ROAD

It might seem like it would be challenging to spend enough time anywhere to establish new relationships when you're constantly on the move. Before we hit the road, Julie was worried that our RV life would consist of a series of repetitive, mundane chitchats with ever-changing temporary neighbors about the weather, where we're from, or what we do. While casual conversation has its place, you, too, may long for more interesting dialogue of greater substance and a sharing of common interests as you had with people back home. While it definitely took some time for us to build friendships on the road, we have found that not only have many of our conversations with other RVers been very enriching, but we've also built a large RVing community and made many close friends on the road.

> "Be prepared for it to change you. For us it was an incredible change for the better, but we've met people who struggled with being in close quarters with their significant others. The experience is amazing. We are now more at peace than we have ever been, relaxed and in tune with ourselves, and well versed in many aspects of America and its people."
>
> —*Jerome Braga, full-time RVer*

Of course, your attitude goes a long way toward making friends on the road and building your RV community. In RVing, just as in life, you'll get out of it what you put into it, and it may take some practice stepping out of your comfort zone to meet new people. If you go out of your way to be friendly and helpful, and introduce yourself and initiate conversations, you're going to have a much easier time—and remember, everyone else is in the same boat! We're all constantly meeting new people every place we go.

Be prepared for your tribe on the road to be more diverse in age and background than ever before. While retired RVing couples may have historically been the largest demographic living on the road full-time, there are increasing numbers of solo RVers, RVing families, and working-age RVers. Keep an open, curious mind when it comes to befriending people of all ages and from all walks of life. This has been one of the things we've loved most about our RV lifestyle—the broad group of fascinating friends we now have and get to reconnect with all around the country.

In our years of full-time RVing this is what we've discovered.

YOU CAN BE YOUR AUTHENTIC SELF

When you live in an area for a long time, those around you often have preconceived ideas about who you are based on where you live and what you do. In the RV world the people you meet tend to have fewer preconceived notions, which can make it a lot easier to be your authentic self. You can just show up, be who you are (or who you want to be), and continue to reinvent yourself as you grow through your travels and experiences.

know people and get right into "real" conversations about any number of topics, as you have nothing to lose. Typically you will either hit it off fairly quickly, or you will be moving on and unlikely to cross paths again.

RVERS ARE FRIENDLY

Generally speaking, most full-time and extended-travel RVers are very open, friendly, and helpful. Perhaps it's because we all realize that we're out here on our own without our usual support network and can use a hand from time to time. RVers are usually more relaxed and engaged, as they aren't caught up with the typical busyness of life. Or perhaps it's because we share the common bond of having stepped out of the box in one way or another, to embrace a life of freedom and travel.

YOU RELATE MORE QUICKLY

Another reason we believe RVers are so welcoming and open is because of the limited time you will likely have together. When meeting people in a campground or on the road you know that you may be in the same area for only a few days or weeks. This allows you to skip over some of the usual steps of getting to

YOU CAN SHARE YOUR EXPERIENCES

Conversations with fellow RVers also tend to be interesting because those who travel a lot usually have great stories to tell and like to share their favorite places to visit and things to do there, along with recommended routes, campgrounds, and restaurants. It's a huge benefit to learn from experienced RVers as you plan your travels to make the most of your journey.

MANY RVERS TRAVEL SEASONALLY

Most RVers travel north in the summer and south in the winter, which increases the density of RVers in certain areas but also keeps you in the best weather. When living in a regular home in an area with cold winters you may hibernate and stay in for the majority of the season, which reduces your social interaction. Winters in the southeastern and southwestern United States tend to be very socially busy times for full-time RVers, as we generally migrate to much warmer areas for longer periods of time, providing more opportunity for being outdoors and connecting with others.

YOU'LL SEIZE THE MOMENT!

The urgency of your encounters also increases the likelihood that scheduled events will happen. Have you ever talked to people you meet in your everyday life who say things like, "We should meet up for dinner or happy hour" only to find it never happens? Well, in the RV world it happens! You realize you have to seize the moment if you want to spend more time with people, as you never know if or when you'll see them again.

YOU'LL ENJOY MORE DIVERSE RELATIONSHIPS

You may also find that your new network of RV friends is more diverse in age, background, and socioeconomics than back in your traditional life. Most relationships in more traditional lifestyles tend to revolve around your neighborhood, work, school, church, or other interests and hobbies, and many of those tend to attract others of a similar age and income level. When RVing there is less separation than is found in traditional neighborhoods, and people spend a lot more time outside, which makes it easier to initiate conversations.

YOU'LL NEED TO BE PATIENT

All this said, you will still need to put in some effort if you want to build relationships. It may take at least a few months before your community on the road starts building and deeper friendships start to take root. Give it time. You're going to meet some amazing people, and they're going to love meeting you too.

BUILDING YOUR RV COMMUNITY—ONLINE AND ON THE ROAD

So where do you go to meet your fellow RVers—or anyone new for that matter—when you're traveling the country in an RV? You'll find them online, offline, in groups, and in places of interest. We've met other full-time RVers sitting next to us at cafés, in restaurants, and even on a cruise ship! But those encounters tend to be more serendipitous.

Here are some of the more common ways to meet people on the road who share your interests, regardless of your age, background, marital status, or sexual orientation.

ONLINE SOCIAL NETWORKS AND APPS

The great thing about online social networks, apps, and communities is that they allow you to start building connections with people well before you hit the road. We've met up with people we connected with via *Instagram*, *Twitter*, our *YouTube* channel, and our *RVLove* blog. There are a ton of interest-based *Facebook* groups out there, like Full-Time RVers, Open Road RV Nomads, Living the RV Dream, RVing in Canada, The RV Entrepreneur, and our own RV Love community, to name a few. The latest, fast-growing community for RVers to connect is the Epic Nomad TV (ENTV) app, which gives you instant access to a fantastic, engaged community of like-minded RV nomads and content creators to connect with in various groups, including our own RVLovers group. The ENTV app gives you your own social profile and delivers streaming content, including the *RV Nomads* movie (watch for free at http://watch.epicnomadtv.com) and more. We'll discuss these further in Chapter 7.

There's also a free social network and app called RVillage.com with more than 100,000 members that allows you to connect online with other RVers and get together at live events. You can "check in" and share your loca- tion, making it easy to connect with others in the same area. You create a name and profile, and can view the profiles of other RVers, which allows you to seek out people with shared interests (motorcycling, boondocking, quilting, photography—anything goes) and find like-minded people in your RV park or area who you can reach out to and meet up with in person. Once you start connecting and making friends within RVillage.com, you can also use the platform to map your travels and keep an eye out for any RVing friends who may be situated along your route, providing even more opportunities to meet up.

Put yourself out there. If you're introverted or shy, it may be easier to build online friendships first, and once you've made connections, it's easy to stay in touch and follow each other's travels through social media, which can lead to in-person meetings when in the same area.

RV MEMBERSHIP SOCIAL CLUBS

There are a number of RV membership clubs that offer support, community, and social events for RVers. The best known are Escapees, Xscapers, FMCA, and the Explorer RV Club of Canada. We'll cover RV membership clubs and their benefits in more detail in Chapter 9, but here's a quick overview of the social and community aspect.

- **Escapees** (www.escapees.com) has been around since the late 1970s and is best known for providing support and community to more than 60,000 RVers—full-timers, part-timers, and weekenders. Members are affectionately referred to as SKPs and the club has many active social communities—online and offline—and runs regular events. Escapees offers Head Out Programs (HOPs) with coordinated tours and outings, travel groups, and local chapters and RV rallies. You can also join Birds of a Feather (BOF) special interest groups around any number of interests and activities, or start one of your own. They are known among RVers as a very friendly and supportive community.

- **Xscapers** (www.xscapers.com) is an RV lifestyle group that was created within Escapees in 2014 to meet the needs of the new generation of RVers with a passion for an active and free-spirited life of travel and adventure while enabling their dreams of working and sharing life on the road. Xscapers welcomes full-time, part-time, and casual RVers, families, couples, and solos of any age. We've met many great friends through the Xscapers community, where the people are helpful, friendly, and fun. Their events (known as convergences) allow RVers to meet up, camp together, work, hike, socialize, and learn from each other. They also have an active *Facebook* page (www.facebook.com/Xscapers) and app.

- **FMCA** (https://site.fmca.com) was originally called the Family Motor Coach Association, but it's now just known as FMCA and is open to all owners of motorized and towable RVs. It is a long-standing RV membership organization with more than 140,000 RVing members that organizes two large national conventions each year, and has several local chapters around the country that put on smaller-scale area rallies with activities throughout the year, like campfires and potlucks. FMCA also has a program where members volunteer assistance and hospitality to other members with their Stop Over Spots, Come Visit, and Mechanic's Helper initiatives, to help fellow RVers traveling through.

- **The Explorer RV Club of Canada** (www.explorer-rvclub.com) is the largest national Canadian RV club serving all members, no matter if you've got a luxury motorhome or a simple pop-up camper. The club organizes rallies and events, offers a range of benefits (more about these in Chapter 9), and is open to anyone living or traveling in Canada, providing the opportunity to connect with others in the great white north! They also have a *Facebook* page (www.facebook.com/ExplorerRVClub).

RV RALLIES

Another great way to meet and socialize with other RVers, RV rallies are organized events that are often hosted by large organizations or clubs with broad membership bases (as mentioned earlier) like Escapees and FMCA, which host national events, conventions, and rallies offering education, entertainment, and community building for RVers. Many RV rallies are also organized by RV owners' groups and manufacturers, which automatically creates additional common ground where attendees who have similar RVs can share knowledge and experience.

RV OWNERS' GROUPS AND FORUMS

These are usually specific to your particular brand of RV and are a great way to connect with fellow owners of similar RVs so you can share information that may be exclusive to those RVs. Active and engaged groups can be a wealth of information and help you troubleshoot challenges and fix them yourself without needing to hire professionals. They also might organize rallies and events, sometimes co-hosted by the manufacturers, that include catered meals and discounted or free repairs on RVs for attendees.

SPECIAL RV-CENTRIC EVENTS

There are many popular events that can be great ways to meet fellow travelers:

- The world-famous Albuquerque International Balloon Fiesta is very popular and a spectacular sight to see.

- The inaugural NomadFEST (www.epicnomadtv.com/nomadfest) brought more than 500 RVers to the town of Wellington, Texas, in October 2018 for a multiday event with BBQ, live music, the premiere of the *RV Nomads* movie, a short film festival, and content creators' conference. Organizers are already planning more Nomad-FEST events for the future.

- The town of Quartzsite in the Arizona desert is famous for attracting thousands of RVers to boondock on free public land in the winter, with gem and mineral shows, an RV show, and a big tent with vendors. Quartzsite attracts hundreds of different RV interest groups, including Escapees, Xscapers, FMCA, RV brand-specific rallies, vintage bus conversions, and the Rubber Tramp Rendezvous (RTR) community, many of them vanners. RTR focuses on frugal RV living and helping those less fortunate, including those who live in an RV because it's their most viable option for living affordably, and now attracts thousands of RVers every year. (Learn more about RTR at www.cheaprvliving.com/gatherings.)

WORKAMPING

If you are looking for something to do and/or ways to camp for free, you might consider doing some work camping, also known as workamping. We'll talk more in Chapter 7 about workamping as it relates to income, but many RVers enjoy workamping as a way to increase their social interaction with other people, especially RVers.

GROUPS RELATED TO YOUR INTERESTS

As you travel, seek out groups or classes on things that interest you. Look for ways to combine your RVing goals with your goals for building community. If your goal is to exercise more, find a hiking buddy to join you. If you're starting a new business, you can connect with one of the many online groups of fellow digital nomad entrepreneurs.

FINDING SPECIFIC COMMUNITIES

No matter what your interests, age, or traveling style, you can find a group of like-minded people if you choose. Here are some common groups and resources for each.

information and organize doggie meetups. There's also Camping and RVing with Pets on *Facebook*.

http://tailsfromtheroad.com, which also has a *Facebook* page (www.facebook.com/RVingwithdogs), to share useful

park or simply while out walking your dog. You can also join groups that connect pet owners online and offline, like

nities to connect with others. You may meet fellow pet owners at an off-leash dog area within an RV

CAMPGROUNDS AND RV PARKS

Many campgrounds organize activities, social gatherings and potlucks to get people together. Once you start looking, you'll find plenty of opportunities out there! You might also find, as we did, that belonging to membership-based campground networks increases your odds of seeing the same people as you travel, as most RVers tend to follow the weather and because other members of that network will usually prefer to stay in network campgrounds to save money.

PET-RELATED EVENTS

Whether it is your pet or somebody else's, furry friends—especially dogs—tend to create opportu-

Whether it's dancing, golf, hiking, motorcycling, quilting, entrepreneurship, or wine tasting—anything goes, and you'll find like-minded RVers along the way.

SOLO RVERS

There are thousands of solo RVers and many more who would like to join them but who may have concerns about feeling safe and being lonely. And while this is a big concern for women, ironically we've met many many more solo RVing women than men, and they are out there thriving! If you're traveling solo, you can meet RVers in every place we've mentioned here, as well as in groups focused on connecting solo RVers, such as LonersonWheels.com, RVingWomen.org, and the Wandering Individuals Network (WIN)—a travel club for single RVers at RVSingles.org. You'll also find solo RVer groups on RVillage.com and as subgroups of RV membership clubs.

RVING FAMILIES

As mentioned in this chapter, there is a large, engaged community of full-time RVing families that offers support, social events, and activities. You can also meet them in campgrounds, RV parks, RV events, and rallies—join them at FulltimeFamilies.com.

WORKING-AGE RVERS

There is a thriving community of digital nomads living from their RVs while working remote jobs, building businesses, or finding work as they travel. Find them at Xscapers.com, at EpicNomadTV.com, and in *Facebook* groups like The RV Entrepreneur.

FRUGAL RVERS

There is a huge community of people who live on the road extremely frugally, many of whom learn from the information, forums, and education shared on the *Cheap RV Living* blog run by Bob Wells, a longtime RVer and van dweller. The related RTR (Rubber Tramp Rendezvous) event began in Quartzsite, Arizona, in 2010 with forty-five people and has exploded in popularity over the years, with around 3,000 people attending in 2018. Once considered the Burning Man for retirees, it's now known for being an accepting and helpful community that attracts people of all ages and walks of life.

LGBTQ RVERS

Members of the LGBTQ community can seek out, connect, meet, travel, and camp with fellow RVers at regular events organized by RainbowRV.com, North America's largest gay and lesbian RV and camping club. You can seek out gay and lesbian RV parks and campgrounds from their website, and join groups like LGBTQ on RVillage.com.

STRIKING UP CONVERSATIONS WITH OTHER RVERS

If you're not a naturally outgoing person, you might need a little help starting a dialogue with people you meet. It is easier than you might think to form deep, lifelong friendships as an RVer. It may not happen right away, but it's surprising just how much the common thread of the nomadic life that we've chosen to live can bond us. Even though many of us will travel throughout the year and may go many months or even years between reconnecting in person, we tend to easily pick up where we left off. Plus, of course, social media makes it easy to stay in touch in the meantime. We've made many deep friendships on the road that we know will last a lifetime.

Here are some ideas for making the process seem less daunting.

USE ICEBREAKERS

You'd be amazed by how many opportunities there are to break the ice and open a dialogue with a complete stranger as an RVer. Often it's something as simple as placing a welcome sign displaying your names and where you are from out in front of your RV. A conversation may kick-start from a travel map displayed on the outside of your RV with stickers showing the states you've visited so far. And there are literally hundreds, if not thousands, of types and brands of RVs out there. You can simply ask people how they like their RV, or be curious and ask specific questions to learn more about it. More often than not people are happy to open up a dialogue about their RV, even if it is a short one. We have found it's generally very easy to start up a conversation with folks because there is almost always something to talk about, and there's usually more time to chat.

SLOW DOWN

Adjusting your travel pace is a big one. It may seem obvious, but it is much easier to meet people and build connection if you are staying in the area longer compared to if you're on the move every few days. Not only will you have more opportunities to make connections, but it will also allow for multiple meetups before you leave the area.

BE OPEN TO SERENDIPITY

As we mentioned earlier, some of the best connections happen when you least expect it. We've met people by striking up a conversation with folks at the table next to us in a restaurant, while traveling in a cruise ship elevator, and answering the inevitable "Where are you from?" question. We even met a new friend while we were all taking selfies with our Mini Coopers at Bixby Bridge near Big Sur, California. You just never know when you're going to meet someone new, and as RVers, we find we stay more open to that than most.

MAKE THE EFFORT

If you just sit around waiting for people to come to you, you probably won't make many friends. If, however, you are willing to put some time and effort into building your community, you will be rewarded with an amazing group of like-minded people who share a spirited sense of adventure, freedom, and fun. Remember, they also had the courage to radically change their life by stepping out of the box, to explore the country by RV.

VOLUNTEERING AS AN RVER

If you're looking for ways to contribute your time in meaningful ways while building community, volunteering is a wonderful way to give back, provide purpose, help others, meet people, and get a free campsite. Volunteering is very popular among RVers, and there are plenty of ways you can participate, depending on your interests and availability.

Mike, Si, and Dawn, ss

FULL-TIME RVERS SINCE JANUARY 2017

Website: www.randombitsoftrialanderror.com

YouTube: RandomBitsRV

Instagram: @randombitsrv

Twitter: @RandomBitsRV

RVillage: RandomBitsRV

"The RV lifestyle not only provides changes in location and beautiful scenery, but it also broadens our minds to new experiences, gives us focus on what's truly important, and feeds our need to wander."

MIKE AND I WERE HUSTLING TO THE TUNE OF THE SOCIETAL "norm." We worked long hours every day only to go to bed, wake up, and do it all over again. Maintaining the big house, having the newest cars in the garage, and collecting newfangled things were all motivation for working harder toward the appearance of being successful. It was exhausting, and we were unhappy. On a family vacation to the shore of Lake Michigan we both felt the unremitting desire to travel more. Mike asked if I would be interested in moving into an RV to travel while working. My response was an emphatic, "Yes! Let's do it."

Since we both worked remotely, we thought the process would be simple. Mike is a cellular network connectivity engineer for one of the largest cellular companies in the US and got approval from his employer right away, but mine flatly refused. I was three years away from thirty years of service and being able to draw an employer-paid pension, so my future retirement date was our goal to begin full-time RVing. Those three years were a flurry of activity.

Finally, our first day of full-timing arrived. We were waylaid by a minor mechanical issue and spent our first night in a Cummins repair facility—an official baptism into the RV lifestyle. Once we hit the first ribbon of highway and started our adventure, we never looked back.

There were no regrets about leaving our stationary life and the vast number of needless things weighing us down. We were light and carefree—and blazing our own trail of freedom.

We quickly learned that full-time RVing is not a perpetual vacation. We're thankful for Mike's steady income to support our expenses, as it allows Dawn to work as a freelance writer, blogger, and virtual assistant. Problems pop up, unexpected expenses occasionally set us back, and family issues occur that need our attention. Real-life problems still exist, but we have the luxury of deciding on our next location, experiencing places we always wanted to explore, and meeting new friends along our journey.

The nomadic lifestyle has changed us. Our goals have become vastly different, from living in a house and staying in one place to no longer striving to collect more things and being slaves to the societal idea of success. Instead we have gathered experiences, have deepened our relationships with family and friends, and continue to make beautiful memories to last a lifetime. We have fed the wandering needs of our souls, and the payback is being happy, relaxed, and fulfilled. We are living our own definition of freedom and enjoying life to the fullest.

You may be drawn to volunteer efforts in a particular geographic region, seeking out opportunities to volunteer at national, state, and city parks and related facilities. Check out America's Natural and Cultural Resources Volunteer Portal at www.volunteer.gov for more information.

Or you may prefer to travel to help out with specific causes, such as:

- Building projects for Habitat for Humanity (www.habitat.org/volunteer/travel-and-build/rv-care-a-vanners) through its Habitat for Humanity RV Care-a-Vanners program.

- Helping with Red Cross DOVE programs (Disaster Operations Volunteer Escapees—www.dovebof.org), which helps with Red Cross projects.

- There are also many faith-based ministries that enable RVers to serve by sharing their time and skills with projects, churches, nonprofits, and local neighborhoods, run by groups such as NOMADS (Nomads on a Mission Active in Divine Service—www.nomadsumc.org) and SOWER (Servants on Wheels Ever Ready—www.sowerministry.org). Working alongside others to help worthy causes, places, and communities is a powerful way to feel like you're making a difference and building some deep relationships through shared time and values.

Some camp hosting positions can also be considered a form of volunteering. We'll talk more about this in the section about work camping in Chapter 7.

CHAPTER 6

LIVING FIT AND HEALTHY ON THE ROAD

Being Your Best Self

"It is no measure of health to be well adjusted to a profoundly sick society."
—*Jiddu Krishnamurti, philosopher*

Deciding to live and travel full-time in an RV can be one of the best things you'll ever do for your overall health and well-being, as it offers significant mental, emotional, and physical benefits. Reducing stress while improving your diet and increasing your exercise are among the best ways to stay healthy, and full-time RVing can help you focus on those goals.

While you get to take greater control over your health and well-being, you still need to navigate the complexities of the confusing and ever-changing healthcare system. We'll keep things fairly simple in this chapter to give you a basic understanding and overview of your options.

MEDICAL AND HEALTH INSURANCE

As you start considering your options for the RV lifestyle, navigating health insurance and medical care may be one of your biggest concerns. There is no single easy answer to this ever-changing conundrum, but there are ways to manage your health needs as an RVer. Health insurance is ultimately all about managing risk and protecting yourself from major incidents and significant expense. Some things may change in relation to the health insurance and plans you are used to, but by understanding your options you will soon discover ways to manage both your expectations and your health.

You may already be on Medicare (or approaching eligibility); you may be employed and covered under your employer-sponsored health plan (or not); or perhaps you are self-employed, self-insured, or mostly managing your own healthcare and simply meeting the basic legal requirements. No matter where your insurance is coming from, you will need to be more proactive in taking responsibility for your health as an RVer, as you'll regularly be on the move and not always able to rely on your primary healthcare providers. We'll talk more about managing your own health in a bit. First, let's take a look at the most commonly used options for medical and healthcare.

WHAT ARE YOUR MEDICAL AND HEALTHCARE OPTIONS?

Understand that the options and costs for health insurance or healthcare plans are going to be different for everyone and will depend on your eligibility, needs, and risk tolerance. When you think about getting health insurance, don't think about it in terms of having your every medical expense covered so much as an insurance policy that is protecting your assets—your health and finances. Health insurance is designed to protect you from the serious financial impact of a health issue (e.g., major surgery, hospital stay, disability), and you can reduce your premiums with a deductible, coinsurance, or a copay. Of course, you should always shop around to compare prices and find savings on your plans, and you can adjust coverage, deductibles, and premiums to find the best fit for you.

Keep in mind that even if you are employed and have a company HMO or PPO health insurance plan, you may not be covered if you're traveling out of your local area. Many plans are regional, and HMOs cover emergency services only when outside of your network. A PPO plan offers better coverage for out-of-network providers.

MEDICARE COVERAGE

If you're eligible, a Medicare card is one of your best, most affordable options for portable health insurance. You can add a supplemental plan to fill in the gaps if necessary. Fortunately for RVers on Medicare and Medigap plans, your coverage is nationwide so you can use it just about anywhere in the US. As Medicare doesn't have "in-network" or "out-of-network" benefits, you'll find that no matter where you travel, you will generally get care at the same level.

AFFORDABLE CARE ACT (ACA) COVERAGE

Otherwise known as Obamacare, this is major medical health insurance from Healthcare.gov or your state's exchanges. However, this system continues to change fast and often, and it is becoming increasingly difficult to find a nationwide PPO coverage option on the Marketplace exchange. There is little point in covering this in much detail, as it will likely have changed again by the time you read this. However, if you are able to find one of these plans, you have a preexisting health condition, and/or you qualify for a subsidy, then this may be an option worth considering.

HEALTH PLANS FOR WORKING AND SELF-EMPLOYED RVERS

In 2018 new ACA-compliant plans were introduced for individuals and families working thirty or more hours per week (through an employer or if self-employed) that are available and provide coverage in all fifty states. You will need to be healthy (no recent or planned surgeries) and not on any expensive medications. These plans are not age-rated, enrollment is open year-round, and they offer nationwide coverage with a large network.

If you are self-employed, you may also be able to start your own small business group plan. A specialized insurance agent or broker, such as RVerInsurance.com, can be helpful in guiding you through this.

HEALTH SHARE PROGRAMS

An alternative used by many RVers is joining one of the ACA-exempt health share programs, sometimes called Healthcare Sharing Ministries (HCSMs). These aren't offered by insurance companies but are run by qualifying organizations that are set up as a nonprofit, so they don't fall under state and federal health insurance regulations. Members pay a monthly contribution that is used to pay qualified medical expenses of other members—so it's a cost-sharing program, not an insurance plan. These are often half the price or less of an unsubsidized health insurance policy, as they are not required to cover preexisting conditions for at least a year or two (i.e., the people joining these plans are usually much healthier than those on health insurance).

There are important caveats: these plans generally do not cover cancer for the first year, and most have a life-time cost-sharing limit of $1 million. Most health share programs are offered by faith-based groups, which often have additional rules around smoking, alcohol, and drug use. Some are Christian-based, while others are non-denominational, but either way, you must sign a statement of faith, so be sure you read the requirements carefully so you understand any restrictions. We pay about $350 per month for the two of us through Liberty HealthShare (www.libertyhealthshare.org), and so far we've been very happy with it, but we're generally healthy, don't take medications, and rarely make claims.

Healthcare Basics: What Do You Need?

When assessing your healthcare needs there are a few key things you need to look for in finding a suitable solution for your traveling lifestyle. You will want:

☐ A network or program that will cover you in the areas where you plan to travel

☐ An insurer or program that doesn't require you to live in your domicile state for a certain amount of time each year

☐ An online or telephone service that offers access to doctors for basic healthcare, like prescriptions and diagnosing common illnesses (like flu, respiratory infections, etc.)

Finally, keep in mind that if you plan to change your state of domicile, you will want to pay close attention to their laws around healthcare, as some states may not offer suitable options for your needs. It's frustrating, we know, but this is an important area where you just have to do your homework, as things are always changing and everyone's needs are different.

SHOP AROUND FOR BEST PRICES

No matter what program or insurance policy you settle on, be sure to compare prices of procedures or treatments at various locations beforehand. For out-of-pocket medical expenses you can often negotiate a much-reduced rate by shopping around for "fixed cash pricing." Use the Healthcare Bluebook (www.healthcarebluebook.com) for a guide on what you can expect to pay for health treatments and procedures in your area, and when calling around to doctors and healthcare providers always ask to have all fees included in the quote. You can save hundreds or thousands of dollars by doing this and may even be able to get a further discount if you prepay, so ask! Be sure to ask about any prescription medications you may need as part of your treatment or recovery and shop around for those, too, as prescription prices can also vary widely.

TAKE CARE OF THESE HEALTHCARE ITEMS BEFORE YOU GO

Before you head out on the road full-time, it's a good idea to get your healthcare materials in order.

COLLECT YOUR MEDICAL RECORDS

Before hitting the road obtain copies of your medical records from your regular doctor if you can, so that you can have them available when visiting any new doctors, or if you choose to set down roots again in a new area. It's a good idea to digitize these to keep them safe and accessible at all times, and these digital versions may remove or reduce your need to bring printed copies.

FILL PRESCRIPTIONS AND MEDICATIONS

If you're on prescribed medications, it's always a good idea to stock up before you leave. Your primary physician should also be able to write prescriptions for you and send them to the local branch of a national pharmacy chain so you can pick up your medications wherever you are. Some prescriptions and prescription plans even allow you to purchase a several-month supply so you don't have to worry about refilling again for a little while.

Once you're out on the road, you can find another local branch of a national chain or get medicine delivered somewhere close to your current location. For example, many RVers have their medicines shipped to RV parks, campgrounds, or a local UPS or FedEx store for collection.

WHAT HAPPENS IF YOU GET SICK?

How do you handle illness, health conditions, or even surgery when you're traveling? Depending on the seriousness or urgency of the situation, you have quite a few options.

TELEPHONE OR ONLINE DOCTOR CONSULTATIONS

Many ailments can be handled via a simple phone call or a virtual consultation online with a doctor who can diagnose health conditions and even prescribe medications, through services like RVHealth.com, Teladoc.com, MDLive.com, and DoctorOnDemand.com. We are enrolled in RV Health but haven't had a need to use it yet. You can get a one-month trial for $1.00 at www.rvhealth.com/rvlove.

TREATMENTS AND CHECKUPS

We've met RVers who are undergoing treatment for certain health conditions and return home periodically for appointments and checkups with their regular providers. You may need to do the same, planning your healthcare needs in advance and scheduling your travels around them. If you spend a lot of time in certain states—say, winter in Arizona or Florida—it's a good idea to start building relationships with healthcare providers in those areas.

URGENT CARE AND ER

It is estimated that about 80 percent of ER visits can be treated at one of the 7,000 urgent care clinics around the country. Most of these are open seven days per week (usually until seven p.m.) and take walk-ins. Head to urgent care facilities for issues such as influenza, minor injuries, bites, stings, burns, sprains, asthma, bronchitis, infections, bleeding (needing stitches), vomiting, diarrhea, and dehydration. Some urgent care clinics even do X-rays. However, not all facilities treat everything, so check the website first or call ahead beforehand.

Of course, if you are experiencing a life-threatening medical problem—like chest pain, stroke, or loss of consciousness—call 911 immediately for care at the nearest emergency room.

SERIOUS ILLNESS, LONG-TERM TREATMENT, AND SURGERIES

For bigger health issues, such as serious illness, hospitalization, long-term treatment, or surgeries, you will need to stay in an area for an extended period of time. In this case, you might choose to return to your hometown to see your regular doctors and have the support of family and friends. You can also use your mobility to your advantage by researching to seek out the best healthcare providers for your situation and then traveling to them. Our full-time RVing friend Greg needed major surgery involving a knee replacement and total leg reconstruction and wanted a highly specialized surgeon to increase his chances of being able to walk afterward. He did his research, found the best surgeon for the job, and traveled to Denver, where he spent a couple of months in a local RV park to have the surgery and focus on recovery and rehabilitation, resulting in a successful outcome.

WHAT IF POOR HEALTH FORCES YOU OFF THE ROAD?

There may come a day when an illness is severe enough to force you off the road, whether for only a few months or longer than that. Depending on the situation, you may still choose to live in your RV during that time, or you may choose to return to a traditional home.

If your illness, the illness of a loved one, or even a loss of interest brings you back to a traditional lifestyle, you can always take a break from RVing and try it again later.

TAKING A PROACTIVE APPROACH TO YOUR HEALTH

As an RVer, you'll be learning to be self-sufficient in ways you may have never been before. Your healthcare and overall well-being truly depend on you taking personal responsibility for yourself. As every person's health needs are different, you need to be willing to take a good look at your own health situation and decide what is going to be the best course of action for you. Here are some of the ways that we, and many other RVers, take a proactive approach to our own healthcare out on the road.

EDUCATE YOURSELF AND PREVENT ISSUES

Nobody is more interested and invested in your health than you, and you can troubleshoot a lot of health concerns with some self-education and preventative measures. As you will constantly be on the move, you will be exposed to new environments and different climates, and the travel itself can take a toll. It may sound obvious, but you really need to pay attention to how you're feeling, listen to your body, and try to nip warning signs and symptoms in the bud quickly, instead of waiting until they catch up with you. This is important not only for your own health and well-being but also for those living in small quarters with you. If you're feeling tired or unwell, rest. If you're feeling the impact of high altitude or a dry climate, stay well hydrated or even relocate if it's affecting you badly. If you have allergies (say, to pollen), be mindful of the peak seasons for those allergens in the regions you travel to, and carry allergy medications with you. Remember, you're in control of your life and schedule and get to choose your destinations, so if certain areas or seasons cause discomfort or trigger health issues, make a change and adjust route planning and timing for future visits, or avoid altogether if needed.

RESEARCH TO FIND A GOOD PRACTITIONER

You may have a good primary care physician back at home, but it's much harder to keep up that relationship when you're on the road. Good doctors can be hard to find, many have a long waiting list, and most aren't interested in developing a relationship with a "transient" person who they may never see again. Don't be concerned—when RVers need a provider, we often use online review sites to find well-reviewed practitioners around the country. In 2016 Marc became ill while we were in Phoenix, and we found a national network with fifty locations called One Medical (www.onemedical.com) that offered same-day, in-person consultations, centralized online records, and a 24/7 online booking system. They can treat common medical issues via phone, app, or online, thus allowing the relationship to continue as we travel.

TRY DIY DIAGNOSIS AND NATURAL HOME REMEDIES

At the first sign of symptoms many RVers jump onto the Internet to try to determine what's going on and find a treatment. We do that, and more often than not we're able to resolve health issues quickly, either with items we have on hand in the RV or a quick trip to the supermarket or pharmacy. We'll often do a *Google* search, refer to the Symptom Checker at WebMD.com, or visit EarthClinic.com for natural remedies that have been tried, tested, and recommended by their community. It's amazing how many ailments can be fixed with simple things that we already have in the RV.

NATURAL REMEDIES FOR COMMON ISSUES

- ☐ Apple cider vinegar—can reduce itchiness of bug bites and relieve acid reflux
- ☐ Hydrogen peroxide—can be used as a mouthwash, or in the ear for earache and colds
- ☐ Iodine—can clean out cuts
- ☐ Baking soda—can reduce heartburn and indigestion
- ☐ Honey—soothes a sore throat, and local honey can help with allergies
- ☐ Lemon—can relieve cold symptoms
- ☐ Aloe vera—can soothe sunburn
- ☐ Essential oils—peppermint and lavender can alleviate headaches; bergamot can reduce fever and treat digestive problems

INVEST IN SIMPLE, INEXPENSIVE HOME TESTING AND HEALTH DEVICES

You can buy simple and cost-effective home testing kits for things like measuring your blood pressure and monitoring your glucose levels to stabilize your blood sugars and reduce the risk of diabetes.

We even purchased a small laser therapy device that offers multiple health benefits, such as relieving acute and chronic pain, helping migraines, reducing inflammation, and healing injuries. It's portable, convenient, and it works!

CONDUCT BLOOD TESTS AND SKIN CHECKS

You can order blood tests for general wellness online for under $100 from companies like DirectLabs.com—you simply order the test you want online, print out the form, and go to your nearest lab for the blood draw, and within a couple of days your results arrive by email. You can also do testing for cardiovascular, heart health, cancer, diabetes, and much more, and you will find better value dealing with independent labs than going through a hospital or doctor's office.

As you travel it's also worth keeping an eye out for free screenings at places like health fairs and expos, or in the pharmacy sections of national chains. Since you'll be spending a lot more time outside (hopefully wearing sunscreen and hats), visit skin cancer clinics to keep an eye on moles and zap precancerous cells as soon as you can.

CONSIDER ALTERNATIVE TYPES OF HEALTHCARE AND HOLISTIC PRACTITIONERS

During our travels we have found affordable chiropractic care at independent chiropractic offices or national networks like The Joint (www.thejoint.com), which has more than 400 locations nationally. We've also visited acupuncturists, Chinese medicine practitioners, homeopaths, and massage therapists around the country, which we usually find through online review sites.

Some years ago Julie had some health concerns that our regular doctor was not very helpful with, focusing solely on the symptom and recommending surgery. By taking initiative and working with an alternative practitioner who delved more deeply into the cause, Julie changed her diet, added some nutritional supplements, and was able to completely heal her health issue and related symptoms, which have never returned to this day. As a result, Julie was able to avoid painful, expensive surgery and months of recovery and physical therapy. It may not be for everyone or every condition, but keeping an open mind to alternative therapies can save you money and help you avoid the need for expensive treatments and medications.

Keep a First Aid Kit On Hand

It's a good idea to keep a simple first aid kit in your RV and your tow vehicle to take care of simple things. Fill it with the basics, like:

- ☐ Aspirin
- ☐ Ibuprofen
- ☐ Adhesive bandages of various shapes and sizes
- ☐ Gauze rolls
- ☐ Antibiotic ointment
- ☐ Tweezers
- ☐ Allergy medication
- ☐ Iodine
- ☐ Ice packs
- ☐ Heat packs
- ☐ First aid tape
- ☐ Alcohol wipes
- ☐ Saline solution
- ☐ Eye drops
- ☐ A thermometer

SEE IF MEDICAL TOURISM MIGHT WORK FOR YOU

If you're willing to travel internationally, you can save up to 90 percent on medical expenses. Medical tourism is booming, with around one million North Americans traveling outside of the US each year for medical treatments in Europe, Asia, and South America, often combining treatment with a vacation. The most common procedures include cosmetic surgery, dentistry, and heart surgery. Among full-time RVers it's common to take a trip down to Mexico for dental work, where hundreds of dentists in several border towns cater to the needs of Americans and Canadians. It is estimated that more than 3,000 people per day walk across the border from Yuma, Arizona, to Los Algodones, Mexico, known as the "dental capital of the world," to visit any one of their 300+ dentists spanning three or four blocks.

While initially nervous, we did extensive research, selected a reputable dentist, and walked across the border to experience Mexican dental work for ourselves. We soon realized that we were very safe in capable hands and a spotlessly clean facility, and paid a fraction of the price it would cost in the US. You can also get prescription eyeglasses and even prescription medications in Mexico, but you should check with Customs and Border Protection (www.cbp.gov) on what you can and can't bring back into the US.

CREATING HEALTHY ROUTINES AND HABITS

We've met many people on the road who made the decision to unplug from their regular lives and began RVing as a way to restore their mental, physical, and/or emotional health. And while RVing in general is a less stressful lifestyle that offers many health benefits, when you first start out, it can also feel a bit like you're on an extended vacation, and if you're not careful, temptations along the way can really creep up on you. Consider your RV life as a great opportunity to reinvent yourself and create some positive and healthy new habits.

REDUCING STRESS

Think of all the benefits you'll get as a result of unplugging from the daily stressors of your former life. You no longer have to deal with long, stressful commutes, rushing around, or grabbing meals on the go. No more going into the office or dealing with office politics and dramas, less home and yard maintenance…it's a simpler life in general, with fewer expenses and responsibilities. You will have more control over your environment, be able to slow down your life pace, reconnect with nature, and create an environment that optimizes your health. You can choose to spend more time in optimal weather and position yourself in locations that make you happy and feed your soul.

Of course, there will always be some stress associated with your RV life, such as learning to drive your RV, parking it, and getting it set up in campsites, especially when you're new. You'll be trying to understand how your RV works,

WHY I LOVE RVING

Joanne, 60

FULL-TIME RVER SINCE DECEMBER 2011

Facebook: Joanne Shortell
RVillage: beyondskp

"The RV lifestyle has allowed me to have an interesting and engaging life that is worth living."

BEFORE I BECAME A FULL-TIME RVER, I WAS 100 PERCENT disabled due to antidepressants that triggered rapid-cycling, drug-resistant Bipolar II. As a workaholic who could not work anymore, was very ill, and with medicine not helping, I felt like I needed to do something radical. I had to go out and dramatically change my lifestyle.

Before I became disabled, I was high-income earner, making over $150,000 a year in 2005. Now I'm disabled and live on $22,000 a year on Social Security, an 85 percent reduction in income. Today I live in a self-contained Mercedes Sprinter van that I bought new and have driven more than 120,000 miles in the past six years. I travel frugally with an extremely low-carbon footprint, living off-grid, using solar power for cooking and electronics, and using less than 10 gallons of water per week, excluding laundry.

The first year after I left my parents and children all had their hearts in their throats. My parents had been avid RVers for years, but I wasn't doing it the way they did, in RV parks. I had no plumbing, had a composting toilet, and was living off the grid. My children were also understandably concerned, thinking of their mom with a scary psychiatric diagnosis, going out to live alone in deserts and national forests. But within the first year they could all see how much this lifestyle was benefiting me. My family was thrilled at how great this was and how much less they needed to worry about me on the road, compared to

life in a crummy apartment barely getting by on my limited budget.

I did all this with the agreement and cooperation of my psychopharmacologist, who recommended a book about a woman who traveled the world with psychological problems and very little money. I am much healthier now, in remission from Bipolar II for several years. I'm not cured, but I have gone from ultra-rapid cycling to none at all in the past few years, without any medication—just me traveling with my service dog, Cafe.

I found a community of people who were more accepting than the neighborhood I left behind. Realizing you are part of something much bigger than yourself and being well accepted can make you psychologically healthier as well. I feel strongly that people who have succeeded and thrived on the road need to nurture those who are new, as it is so scary and so challenging to give up a normal American life. The online and in-person communities I discovered through Bob Wells at CheapRVLiving.com and the related RTR events are fabulous resources for people who do not have a lot of money or are not doing well living in traditional society.

This is a great way for people to live if they are different and if they need to use the resources they have in a nontraditional way. My mental and physical health have improved immensely, and the lifestyle has been truly life-changing for me.

manage the systems, and handle repairs and breakdowns. You will also be dealing with the emotions that come with big change, leaving behind your community, adjusting to your new home on wheels, and being out of your comfort zone. It's all part of RV life, but when you don't have all of your regular stresses and responsibilities to deal with on top of it, it can be easier to take all of this in your stride. And remember, every aspect of RV life—including learning and growing—is part of the adventure.

It can take time to get used to the change of pace that comes with your new lifestyle. Learning to NOT feel stressed can even take time, as it may have been a running theme in your life for many years. It can be very tempting to get busy and try to be productive all the time. Give yourself time and permission to slow down, relax, and just be for a while. There will always be things to do, but sometimes it takes a while to hit the reset button, as we have been so programmed by society to always be on the go. This is especially true if you've just retired or left a high-pressure job, and of course, there's the adrenalin that comes with the stress and excitement of selling, downsizing, and getting ready to hit the road.

Go easy on yourself and give yourself time to unwind and adjust. Maybe even introduce meditation into your daily routine as you redefine what your days, life, and priorities look like. You may even find that a lot of your health issues and symptoms start improving as the stress slowly starts to dissipate from your life.

HEALTHY EATING

The RV lifestyle can be very social, filled with campfires, s'mores, potlucks, and happy hours. And, of course, you're almost always somewhere new and exciting, which brings with it the temptation to eat out more often, try new restaurants, and taste the local treats and drinks. Not only can eating out get expensive, but it's not usually a recipe for optimal health. If you're not careful, it can be way too easy to pack on the pounds.

COOKING IN YOUR RV

When you live in your RV with your favorite appliances, it's also easy to prepare most of your meals at home, freeze leftovers, and stock your RV with healthy snacks for hiking and picnics, salads, or sandwiches for days when you head out to explore. We always like to have healthy meals ready for travel days or for when we return after a big day out. Sure, we love eating out at restaurants, too, but most of our meals are prepared in our RV kitchen.

While you won't be able to maintain much of a garden while on the road (maybe a few potted herbs if you're lucky), you will be able to visit local growers and farmers' markets offering fresh produce, and have access to quality grocery stores in many cities. You may even find some interesting new foods to try that were not normally available in your old neighborhood stores.

Setting yourself up for success with meals when RVing might involve a little extra planning compared to your traditional home, partly because your pantry and fridge may not be as large, but you can buy an RV with a residential fridge and large pantry if that is important to you. You can visit our RV gear store to see what appliances we use in our RV and kitchen at https://rvlove.com/ShopGear.

MEAL PLANNING

Because you're always on the move and you never know what stores might be in the next town, meal planning is great idea. It keeps you focused on buying only the ingredients you need, maximizes the use of your fridge and pantry space, and saves time and money—all while having better control over your diet. Meal planning is especially important if you have allergies or special dietary needs, as you may need to bulk buy or special order certain ingredients.

Prepare meals in advance for travel days, which can often be tiring, unpredictable, or result in unforeseen delays. Having a ready-made meal that's quick and easy to warm up or eat on your arrival will help nourish you and help you avoid getting "hangry."

SPECIAL DIETS OR INGREDIENTS

If you have allergies or other dietary restrictions, know that it is possible to find what you need on the road. It may take some planning ahead, and your preferred food sources may be more abundant in some places than others, but you should be able find what you need, even if you have to order some products online. Wholesale clubs and grocery chains usually have a good selection of health and organic foods too. We often look online for healthy recipes that call for just the ingredients we have in our RV to keep things simple.

REGULAR EXERCISE

Exercise tends to increase for most RVers because they usually find themselves in good weather—the key is making sure you get out of the RV! If you get too comfortable in your RV and hang out inside most of the time, you will likely walk far fewer steps than you did living in your traditional home because it's a much shorter walk to the bedroom, kitchen, bathroom, and living area.

GET OUTSIDE!

Fortunately, living in an RV makes it much easier to get outdoors for hiking, biking, kayaking, or swimming, as you can park your RV where the weather is conducive to those activities year-round. You will find that simply being in new and interesting places will inspire you to get out and do more, especially if you're going to be in an area for only a short time. If you are going to hike that trail that everyone's been talking about, you need to do it now, not next week! Explore the hiking trails at national and state parks or when you're out boondocking in wide-open space. You'll find local running trails at MapMyRun.com, plus a nationwide network of trails that were formerly rail lines and are fantastic for hiking and biking at RailstoTrails.org.

REIMAGINING TRADITIONAL GYM WORKOUTS

You may have had a gym membership back at home, and you can still visit a national gym chain if your membership allows, but it won't always be convenient to find one nearby. Some RV parks have fitness centers with workout equipment. Packing down and setting up your campsite might be more exercise than you had imagined. You can also do some simple weight-bearing exercises using small hand weights or cans of food. Online yoga and workout sessions are easy to find, too, such as those at www.thefitrv.com/workouts/.

OTHER WAYS TO MOVE

Another way to be sure you get exercise is to look for ways to integrate body movement into your everyday life as much as you can. Try these ideas:

- Incorporate workouts throughout the day. Walk or bike to the campground office or grocery store instead of driving, or park a little farther from the store to get in extra steps. In our RV life, we like to take walks around the campground, hike trails, and use our bikes to explore.

- See what's available where you're staying. Many campgrounds have swimming, tennis, mini golf, shuffle-board, pickleball, basketball, and other activities.

- Wear a step tracker, pedometer or *Fitbit*, or use an app like Stepz, Runkeeper, or Map My Run on your smart-phone to track your activity and nudge you to take those extra steps or walk that extra loop. Whether you're competing with your partner or trying to better your own results from yesterday, these are all little ways to help you move even more.

RVING CAN HELP YOU FORM NEW HABITS

If you haven't made your health and fitness high priorities in your life, transitioning to the RV lifestyle provides the perfect chance to hit the reset button and establish new patterns and habits to support your optimal health and create your best self. Some experts say that it takes only twenty-one days to establish a new habit or life pattern. You get to desire or decide. What is it that you desire in your life? If you want something badly enough, the next step is to shift that desire into a decision. They are similar words, but there is a big difference. When you simply desire something, even small obstacles can seem difficult to overcome, but if you have decided that you are going to make something happen, your mind will immediately search for ways around that obstacle instead of letting it stop you.

Try little experiments in your daily life. You might desire to exercise more often, but your days seem to get away from you and each one ends without it happening. However, if you decide you are going to exercise more often, you will set your alarm a bit earlier in the morning, and the alarm will be across the room so that you have to get out of bed to turn it off. When you walk over to your alarm clock with your exercise clothes sitting beside it, you won't struggle with an internal debate about exercise because you have already decided you are going to make it happen. Maybe

you'd like to stop watching so much TV and do something more productive with your time. The desire to stop watching TV isn't enough because it is fleeting and your habit will see you back on the couch. Once you decide that you are going to stop watching TV, you will unplug or even physically remove the TV from the room, so that it's easier to do something else than to go get the TV and plug it back in. The decisions we make today affect our tomorrow. Whether it is improving your health or changing your life, it's the same principle, just on a bigger scale.

Last but not least, remember that attitude is everything. Keep an open mind and embrace a positive attitude of adventure and curiosity to keep you exploring and moving forward. It will also help challenges roll off your shoulders without stressing you out. As with any major transition, you will always face a few obstacles, but stay optimistic and look for the good in every situation. As Julie's dad always says, "Everything happens for a reason, and it's always for the best." Sometimes it can be hard to see the positive side or the reason for something, but it's in there somewhere. You just never know—that traffic delay might have prevented you from being in the wrong place at the wrong time. Keep things in perspective and roll with it.

WHAT ABOUT PERSONAL SAFETY?

Another topic that is commonly raised by people considering the RV lifestyle is personal safety. We will start by saying we have felt just as safe, or even safer, in this lifestyle than we did in our previous home. In traditional neighborhoods it is sometimes easier for criminals to learn the patterns of behavior of their targets. RV parks have more people living outside and in closer proximity, which translates to more witnesses to suspicious behavior.

With Marc being a former law enforcement officer, perhaps the best advice we can offer is simply not to be a good target. Being aware of your surroundings and keeping items—especially valuable things, like bikes—locked up or at least out of sight will dramatically reduce your risk of being a victim of crime. Secondly, the vast majority of RVers you will encounter are part of a warm, friendly, and helpful community. There is a high percentage of retired (and armed) police, fire, and military personnel out on the road, who generally make poor targets for criminals.

Learn to trust your intuition or your gut feelings. If you pull into a place and something looks suspicious or just doesn't feel right, trust that feeling and do whatever's necessary to make yourself feel more comfortable. Remember that you have wheels, so it's easy to pack up and move to a location where you feel safer.

The Braga Family

(Jerome, 45, Jennifer, 35, Leighton, 9, and Shayla, 7, plus our dog Cole, 10)

WE INITIALLY HIT THE ROAD AS PART-TIME SNOWBIRDS FROM LATE 2015, THEN FULL-TIME FROM LATE 2016

Website: www.our1chance.com
Twitter: @our1chance
Instagram: @our1chance
RVillage: Our1Chance
Facebook: Our 1 Chance

"The most inspirational part of the RV lifestyle is the simplicity of living, coupled with the almost endless exploration options each location has to offer. Traveling to warmer climates prompts us to be significantly more active and physically fit."

OUR ENTIRE RV STORY REVOLVES AROUND OUR BEST EFFORTS TO find a solution to living a fulfilling and adventurous life despite our daughter Shayla's severe food allergy restrictions. We quickly learned that we would never be able to travel and stay in hotels, eat in restaurants, or travel on airplanes as a family. The only way for us to vacation and adventure was by bringing along our own kitchen and living accommodations.

The abridged story found us homeschooling our girls and traveling in our RV across the US. As professional photographers/filmmakers and marketers, we have taken our business mobile and home market of Connecticut during the summers. Although they initially looked like an unmanageable and impossible life hurdle, Shayla's food allergies have given us the gift of family, healthy eating, exploration, and unprecedented life experiences.

Before our RV lifestyle we were living a typical, self-employed American life, working endless hours to grow our business. Freeing ourselves up to live in a smaller space took away all the unnecessary frivolities of modern life. Having fewer expenditures removed the need to incessantly drive our business forward. Finding a peaceful balance is still something we aspire to, but our movement toward that has already improved our physical and mental health and overall quality of life.

By seeking out warmer climates in the RV we can exercise almost daily. When we were back home in Connecticut, the winters would find us indoors, less active, adding weight, and experiencing seasonal depression. In the RV we get to keep up our routine of yoga, Pilates, weights, power walks, hikes, and bike riding, and we often find time in the afternoon for some soul-cleansing exercise.

We renovated our RV kitchen to better suit our needs. We added almost 3 extra feet of counter space and several more kitchen cabinets to help accommodate all the fresh foods and whole ingredients that go into our diets. Most RVs aren't equipped for meal preparation as intense as ours, but after some creative construction we now have the ideal kitchen on wheels.

As a family, we don't require much medical intervention unless Shayla has a severe reaction to something she consumed or catches a cold. As a result, we have adjusted our health and medical insurance to reflect high-deductible major medical coverage. Since we spend winters in warmer climates, Shayla doesn't need to be on her regular preventative asthma medication and is better able to avoid colds, which keeps our trips to the hospital to almost none. Most of her asthma and allergy medications are paid out of pocket; however, with careful management of her exposure to her stressors, we likely save well over $1,500 a month being on the road.

Our RV lifestyle has had so many positive effects on our lives. From the unimaginable amount of family time spent with our girls, to viewing the country's amazing natural wonders, to keeping our daughter safe from exposure to dangerous allergens, to the healthy lifestyle we get to enjoy, RVing has brought us more joy and fulfillment than we could have ever imagined in our wildest dreams.

FIREARMS

While we choose not to carry firearms in our RV—we don't feel the need and find it too limiting for where we want to travel—we know many RVers who do. However, be aware that firearms are not legal in every state and the laws can be very strict, so do your research and understand the gun laws in each state before traveling through, as you may be breaking the law without realizing it. The same goes for traveling into Canada or Mexico—check the laws before you travel.

KNOW WHERE YOU ARE

Most people have their permanent address memorized, but when you move frequently, it is harder to commit your location to memory. That's why it is a good practice to make note of your new location so that it is easy to offer to emergency service providers should an emergency occur. If you are woken up and still half asleep, having it written down in a consistent location will help in sharing your location accurately.

We also recommend that you consider letting somebody back "home" know your new location whenever you move. We always give Marc's mom a call or text her to let her know where we are. It's a great opportunity to check in and say hi and also let her know our whereabouts just in case. You may also want to add your cell phone numbers to a shared app like Find My Phone, Find My Friends, or Glympse, so loved ones can see your whereabouts via GPS.

DEALING WITH WILDLIFE

Whether we're out hiking in national parks like Yellowstone or Glacier, or at home in our RV, we have found that a can of bear spray is handy as a form of protection. It's not as lethal as a firearm, it's legal to carry when you travel, and it's easy to strap to your belt when hiking in bear country. When we're at home in the RV, we use Velcro strips to attach a can of bear spray near the front door of our RV as an effective tool for self-defense if we ever feel we need it, regardless of species!

PART 3

PRACTICAL CONSIDERATIONS

There are many practical puzzle pieces to put in place when it comes to making your RV lifestyle a reality. Remember, you're not just driving off and checking out of life! You are reinventing how you live so you can maximize your freedom, mobility, and travel. You may still have to work (unless you're retired or already financially independent) to fund your lifestyle. Then there's how to navigate all of the legal stuff, like choosing a state of domicile, filing taxes, and voting. And let's not forget taking care of the practicalities of paying bills, banking, and dealing with your mail. You're still an active and participatory member of society; you're just choosing to participate from different locations around the country so you can have more freedom to come and go as you please, enjoy better views, and make the most of your life.

The good news is that once you have all those pieces in place, you get to focus on more of the fun stuff, like travel planning—deciding on where to go and where to stay and discovering new places to explore. These are all pieces of the puzzle that will take some time to navigate as you get properly set up for your transition to RV life. Let's dive in and cover all the most important things you'll need to put in place to make it happen.

HOW TO SET UP A REMOTE ARRANGEMENT

Not all companies are open to this type of remote-working arrangement, especially older companies with a more traditional mindset, but you may find many younger or open-minded companies that are willing to explore the possibility, especially if you've already proven to be a valuable, reliable, and productive employee. We've met people who insisted their employer would never allow it, but after putting together a proposal outlining the benefits and a successful trial period, they got the green light and were able to start doing their jobs from the road. We've also met folks who, as they neared retirement age, approached their employers about starting to transition their career sooner by working remotely, or who shifted to a part-time consulting role after their official retirement date, to continue contributing their skills and expertise. Others have paved the way by getting approval to work remotely while caring for ill or elderly parents; then, after proving their ability to deliver while out of sight, they were able to continue working remotely via RV. And we've met a few whose employers responded to their initial request with resistance but, after being presented with a resignation, came around. The bottom line is that if you're a valued employee, the company may be willing to work with you on finding a remote-working solution to keep you on staff so you can continue contributing your talents and expertise.

During our first two and a half years on the road Marc managed operations for his employer for their (mostly) virtual company, and most of his colleagues didn't even know he lived in an RV, as they never noticed any change in his productivity or availability. We even spent a month in Australia in 2016, and Marc made it work! The hours were brutal (he worked midnight to nine a.m. Australian time to work on US business hours), but it was doable. At the end of the day it doesn't (or shouldn't) really matter to employers as long as their employees are getting their work done seamlessly, as in Marc's case. If you're already working from home, there is really no reason why you can't simply transition your workspace to your RV. And if you don't need to go into an office, does your employer even need to know where you are sitting, as long as you are doing your job?

Of course, you will need to be self-disciplined, make Internet connectivity a priority, and, if you work fixed hours, be willing to adjust your work schedule to ever-changing time zones as you travel, but as long as you continue delivering, there are advantages for both parties.

WORKING A "REGULAR" JOB ON A DIFFERENT SCHEDULE

We've met airline pilots, flight attendants, boat captains, and truck drivers who still work their regular jobs in between RVing. We even met one fellow who works one week on and one week off as a trainer for a company in Alberta, Canada, and in winter flies three hours each way to and from Arizona every other week to join his wife in their RV. These options may require people to situate themselves near major airports, seaports, or other locations as needed, but they find a way to make it work for them.

SELF-EMPLOYMENT

Do you already work for yourself, or are you considering starting a new business? The freedom and flexibility of working for yourself and creating your own schedule are liberating, but it can also actually be harder to take time off. Most entrepreneurs we know put in long hours building their business and may not have the luxury of taking a week or two off to completely unplug. You will need to be able to discipline yourself, and understand that your income can be inconsistent or unpredictable, especially when you're starting out, unless you find a way to transition from a job to self-employment and already have a product or client list lined up with projects or contracts.

If you have an idea for a more lucrative online business, then yes, building your own business online can be a fantastic way to complement your new lifestyle of freedom. Maybe you have a unique skill set that makes you a valuable consultant, or you are really good at finding deals on items and reselling them for a profit. Maybe you are skilled at managing money or doing online trading. Our biggest piece of advice is to wait until there is at least some tangible evidence of the financial viability of that business, unless you are in a financial position that allows you significant time to develop an alternate plan if your first plan doesn't work out. Maybe you have some money put aside that you know you can live on while you work on developing your new business.

If you're already self-employed, and especially if you're working from home, the transition may be easy. Even if you run your own business and have an office and a team, it's still doable. We met an inspiring, solo woman RVer, Lisa, who ran her father's medical weight-loss business in person for ten years. She shifted her thinking and began promoting and empowering her staff to take on more responsibility and run things, and now she lives and travels full-time in her RV, working only a few hours a week.

DON'T BE AFRAID TO GET CREATIVE AND RESOURCEFUL

Remember when we talked about designing your RV life in Chapter 2? If you're struggling to imagine how you could work from the road, try this: combine what you're good at with what you love. Think about the skills and experience you've already developed over the years, as well as the contacts and networks you've made. Reflect on what you really love doing, how you like to spend your time and energy, and the kinds of things you do for free, just because it comes naturally and doesn't even feel like work. If you can find a way to blend your passions with your talents, that's a great place to start thinking about what kind of business or income stream could be a fit for your new life.

Even if you start a business as a small side gig, over time it could grow into a thriving business. For example, when we started *RVLove* in June 2014, Marc was working full-time at his remote job, and Julie was producing most of our content as a fun, creative outlet to help people while sharing our adventures. *RVLove* continued to grow organically over the years, until we reached a perfect storm at the end of 2016. Marc was burned out by his job and ready for a change, and our blog and *YouTube* channel had grown to a point where they needed more focused time and attention, so we decided to direct all of our efforts to *RVLove* full-time. It was a risk, but Marc took the plunge and quit his well-paying job and we placed a bet on ourselves. We were able to use our combined skills and talents, and focus on doing what we loved (which we'd been doing in our spare time anyway). To accommodate the change we slowed down our travels and scaled back our spending. That risky decision paid off, as our business has grown to a level that comfortably supports us, creating more freedom and flexibility in our schedule, and allowing us to spend our time on work that is much more intrinsically rewarding.

> **"What if you started living the way you really want to, instead of the way society thinks you ought to?"**
>
> —*Marc Bennett, coauthor of this book*

One of the greatest benefits to the RV lifestyle for somebody starting a new business is flexibility. For example:

- You can live very inexpensively when income is light, and live a bit more luxuriously once the income is more consistently rolling in.

- You will also have location independence, allowing you to very quickly and easily relocate to an area that is more lucrative for your business, or for your day job as you build a business. This provides greater opportunity for start-up businesses. The more options, the better! People who buy homes in a city generally limit themselves to job opportunities within reasonable commuting distance.

If you're just starting out and you don't already have a nest egg or another source of income to cover your expenses while you're building a new business, entrepreneurialism can be risky, especially if you are relying on this as your primary way to make money when you first hit the road. But then again, isn't it also risky to stay stuck in a job or a life that isn't working for you? Food for thought: What risks are you willing to take to create a life you love? What if you could start something now and see where it takes you?

OTHER WAYS TO MAKE MONEY WHILE TRAVELING

Working-age people have been living and traveling full-time in RVs for decades, but most of them did work that required them to be physically present and often traveled to find employment. Now jobs can be found ahead of time through online research, job boards, and agencies, so you can find jobs in places and at times that suit you first, then travel to do the work. Here are some examples.

WORKAMPING

Also known as work camping, workamping is one of the best-known options for part-time and full-time RVers looking for a way to get a free campsite, earn money, and/or stay busy while meeting new people. Workamping is popular with solo RVers, couples, and families alike, and especially retirees looking for volunteer work as they travel. RVers often tend to seek ways to earn income from the road or look for seasonal work as a way to combine physical activity with a traveling adventure. Workamping roles usually don't pay much, but they almost always offer a free campsite in the park in exchange for a certain number of hours, and some positions also pay hourly wages (usually in the range of $7–$12) and benefits.

Some of the more common positions include campground hosts, greeting new arrivals, working in the office, housekeeping, maintenance, and landscaping. But there are also roles for shuttle bus drivers, park rangers, tour guides, and cooks. Workamping roles also extend beyond RV parks and campgrounds, to places like national and state parks, US Forest Service locations, theme parks, dude ranches, golf courses, lodges, marinas, gift shops, and wildlife refuges, to name a few. You can learn more about workamping, build a resume, and view job listings at web-sites like Workamper.com and WorkampingJobs.com.

TEMPORARY JOBS

There are many temporary roles that can be a great fit for RVers who are willing to take their home on wheels and go to where the work is. Whether it's for just a few weeks or months at a time, you get to choose the type of work, location, and, in many instances, your schedule. Temporary work is common among nurses, building contractors, oil field gate attendants, agricultural workers, and musicians, among others. If you have been laid off from your job or can't find suitable work in your local area, it could also be an ideal time to reframe your situation as an opportunity for trying out the RV lifestyle, as you can travel to find work in other parts of the country and earn money while having adventures along the way.

SEASONAL WORK

There are many more seasonal, hands-on roles that can be filled by a mobile workforce. Tourism and hospitality roles typically have peaks and valleys in staffing needs, often aligning with the best weather for RVers and their typical travel schedule. For example:

- In agriculture, crops have their peak harvest times, like the sugar beet harvest, which takes place in the first three weeks of October between northwestern Montana and northwestern Minnesota. This is popular among RVers who like physical activity, and good money can be made (around $12 per hour). The shifts are long (twelve hours), but some employees can make up to $2,500 in a two-week timeframe. Learn more at www.sugarbeetharvest.com.

- Construction roles often follow the weather and local economic growth.

- Nursing roles (while always in demand) tend to fluctuate as a population ebbs and flows. Some cities in Arizona, Florida, and South Texas, for example, will see their populations shrink by as much as 50 percent when the winter "snowbird" season ends.

- Amazon's CamperForce program hires huge numbers of seasonal employees in the lead-up to their peak shopping season in November and December to work at their nationwide distribution centers. It can be physically demanding work—sometimes involving walking more than 10 miles a day through their distribution centers picking items or packing boxes—but if you are looking to increase your exercise, get a free campsite, and earn some decent money in the process, it might appeal to you. Learn more at www.amazondelivers.jobs/about/camperforce, and search online to read about RVers' experiences with Amazon CamperForce.

Some seasonal roles may provide you with enough income in just a few months to support you for the rest of the year—if you live frugally and prefer to spend the rest of your time traveling—or you may just like the extra boost of cash it brings. More often than not, seasonal workers will take on at least two seasonal roles in a year.

WWOOFING

WWOOF is an acronym that stands for World Wide Opportunities on Organic Farms. WWOOFing involves working at organic farms where you might enjoy learning about farming and watching the fruits (or vegetables) of your labor grow. You get to help out on host farms and learn about organic farming and agriculture in exchange for a free place to park your RV, which may or may not have hookups. WWOOFing gigs usually last from a few days to a few months, and the experience can provide a great learning opportunity, especially for kids. Be aware that some farm owners may expect a lot of hours of physical farm labor for your free site, so you'll have to decide whether that tradeoff works for you. Visit https://wwoofinternational.org to see WWOOFing opportunities around the world and links to WWOOFing websites for different countries.

USE YOUR IMAGINATION!

The range of jobs you can do from the road is truly as unlimited as your imagination. We've met RVers who design T-shirts, transport RVs, design and sell cocktail accessories, run Etsy stores, host websites, fly hot air balloons, work at trade shows, and even do obscure jobs like retrieving golf balls from water features on golf courses using scuba gear. We even know of people who fund their RV travels by securing dog walking jobs using apps like Rover and Wag. Don't limit yourself to the jobs we've mentioned here—these are just a few. Take some time to think about what would be really fun for you, whether it's something you already have experience with or you want to try something new. You don't necessarily need to worry about making as much money as in your current job, especially if you're willing to be flexible and scale back your expenses in order to make the transition. Then again, you could end up finding or creating a new career that is even more lucrative. It's up to you!

SHOULD YOU START A BLOG OR *YOUTUBE* CHANNEL?

Many aspiring RVers first learn about and are inspired to live the RV lifestyle by reading a blog post or watching a *YouTube* video. This is how many people have discovered us and *RVLove*, and it has led to many wonderful new friendships and experiences, a great community, and amazing professional opportunities, like creating our online RV Success School courses, getting involved with the *RV Nomads* movie, and even writing this book!

When we first started out, there were just a handful of RVing blogs and *YouTube* channels consistently sharing quality content, and these were a great source of inspiration and knowledge. Now there are hundreds of RV, travel, and lifestyle-related blogs and channels out there. While some have grown to become very popular and successful, others may launch with a bang and eventually fade away, as it's not always sustainable, personally or financially. Nowadays there's a lot of competition, and it takes real work.

We've had many people tell us they feel they are supposed to start a blog or *YouTube* channel when they start traveling because "that's what everybody does." Before investing the time, energy, and money into creating a blog or *YouTube* channel, ask yourself a few big questions, and reflect on your "why" as you do it.

- **Why do you want to start a blog or *YouTube* channel?** Are you doing it for you, because everyone else seems to be doing it, or because your family members asked you to? Revisit your goals for RVing in the first place and be honest with yourself. It's not for everyone, and you don't need to do both—or either, for that matter.

- **What do you hope to gain from it? Do you have a specific goal?** Is it to share, help, and inspire others? Perhaps your eventual goal is to earn money on the side or create a whole new business. Do you want to gain popularity, recognition, or even fame? Do you want to feel like you belong and join a like-minded community? Do you feel compelled to share your story? Maybe you want to learn new skills or use the ones you already have.

- **Do you have the skills or are you willing to learn?** Blogging requires writing skills, making *YouTube* videos requires video and editing skills, and you'll need to learn technology platforms to do either. Your willingness to learn and grow is more important than having the skills to get started.

- **Are you willing to put yourself out there publicly?** Are you an introvert or an extrovert? Are you comfortable sharing publicly? Do you prefer privacy and anonymity? Do you want to uncover your authentic self, find your voice, or increase your confidence? There's no simple answer, only your honest one.

- **Do you have the time?** If you are traveling full-time, exploring, working, and spending time with your partner or family, how much time will you have left over for writing a blog or making *YouTube* videos? You can't do it all, so what's most important to you?

MANAGING EXPECTATIONS

Blogging and YouTubing can be a part-time or full-time job in terms of how much time it takes, especially if you are using social media to promote your sites. Realistically it's going to take a minimum of a year if you work really hard at it, perhaps two, three, or many more years, to build a blog (and an email list) or *YouTube* channel that will generate enough income to eventually become your primary income stream. Why? It simply takes time to build content and an audience, so you'll need to be patient, and also be prepared for the possibility that it might never really take off or that you may run out of steam, content ideas, money, or all three. But remember, everyone starts with zero subscribers! Measure your success with small, realistic milestones to start with to keep you motivated, and surround yourself with a supportive community so you can cheer each other on. Epic Nomad TV has a great community and resources for content creators, which you can find at http://watch.epicnomadtv.com.

As you grow, you'll probably have to deal with negative comments (or no comments at all) and even trolls attacking you. It's not fun, but it's hard to avoid, especially on *YouTube*, though it seems to be less prevalent on blogs. The most successful bloggers and *YouTube* creators have a real passion for what they do and a love for the content and

Cherie, 45, and Chris, 45

FULL-TIME RVERS FROM 2007 TO 2017 AND NOW SPLITTING TIME BETWEEN RVING AND CRUISING

Website: www.technomadia.com

YouTube: Technomadia

Instagram: @cherie_technomadia and @chris_technomadia

Facebook: Technomadia

"RVing has been an incredible platform for us to explore our wanderlust while being introverted, homebody-natured nomads. We can be exactly where we want to be—whether that's somewhere with an inspiring view or close to loved ones—and always be at home."

AFTER YEARS OF DREAMING ABOUT A NOMADIC LIFESTYLE AND inspired by the original technomad, Steven Roberts, Chris hit the road solo in 2006 in a 16-foot teardrop trailer. Soon after meeting Cherie online, we quickly realized our lives were well aligned in romance, partnership, business, and wanderlust. Cherie was already working remotely running her software development business, and was able to transition fairly easily to a fully mobile lifestyle, assuming we could maintain reliable Internet connections during normal business hours.

The teardrop trailer had just 45 square feet of living space, and no bath facilities, refrigerator, or air conditioning, but we had solar power, cellular Internet, and an exciting new relationship. We learned that was all we really needed to be happy. The following year we commissioned a custom-built, 17-foot fiberglass travel trailer with as much solar and battery capacity as we could squeeze into it, providing us with a luxurious 80 square feet of living space, a bathroom, a refrigerator, and air conditioning. Three years later, our desire for a dual ergonomic workspace to enhance our work productivity led us to buy a 1961 GM 35-foot vintage bus conversion, "Zephyr," which we modified over the years as we traveled to make her our ideal high-tech, decadent home on wheels.

Our primary source of income has been via our tech and consulting company, with projects ranging from mobile app development, technology advising, market research, advising tech start-ups, technical writing, journalism, and orchestrating unique product launch strategies. Our travels have also inspired a line of incredibly useful travel apps to solve problems we encountered on the road.

We've work camped for Amazon's CamperForce program packing boxes during the holiday rush, volunteered full-time to run a presidential campaign field office in rural Nevada, orchestrated a guerrilla marketing launch of the iPhone travel app HearPlanet at Macworld 2009 (involving organizing a weeklong party on a double-decker bus), volunteered as interpretive lighthouse hosts in Oregon, consulted for and helped launch the *RVillage* social network for RVers, and helped the Escapees RV Club return to their roots by launching the Xscapers club-within-a-club to provide content for working-age RVers.

Fast forward several years. After documenting our personal travels and fielding many questions about how we stay connected, we pivoted our careers in 2014 and founded the Mobile Internet Resource Center to help our RVing, cruising, and nomadic communities stay on top of the always-changing options for staying connected. This is now our primary income source and perfectly meshes our passion for the intersection of technology, travel, and serving our community.

Our most memorable travel adventures almost always center around our experiences rather than the places we've visited. But our passions for travel go beyond just exploring North America by land, so our newest chapter is splitting our time between RVing part-time while cruising America's waterways by boat, another form of travel that keeps us always at home while we roam as we work, while always staying connected.

message they are sharing, which is what keeps them going when it gets tough, so check in with yourself and be honest about how much time, energy, and money you're willing to invest.

The bottom line: do your research and ask yourself questions before jumping in with both feet. If you are creating online content with the sole intent of making money, thinking that you will just hit the road and your lifestyle will be fully supported by your earnings from *YouTube*, you're going to be in for a rude awakening. Some *YouTube* channels, even those with thousands of subscribers and hundreds of videos, are barely making enough money to pay for their creators' groceries every month, let alone support their entire lifestyle. You will find a better hourly rate for your time at most any other job, but if you have the time and passion for it, and are already earning enough to support your basic needs, it can also be very rewarding in many other, non-financial ways.

As you will learn from the RVers featured in this chapter, if you have the desire, it is definitely possible to create an income from blogging or YouTubing; just find your niche, keep creating quality content, work hard, and be patient!

INTERNET SOLUTIONS

Being able to access the Internet is essential for just about everyone these days, no matter where you are. Technology makes it easier for RVers to live mobile, whether it's so you can use your GPS, search for local services, bank online, read restaurant reviews, find a supermarket or post office, or seek out campgrounds and the best fuel prices. Then there's email, social media, video calls with family and friends, and being able to use apps for just about every aspect of our lives. And for those of us who need to work, run a business, or find work, having a reliable Internet connection could be considered even more important than having hookups at a campground! It's entirely possible for us to fill our tanks, fire up our generator or be powered by our batteries and solar panels, while we are out boondocking in the middle of nowhere, as long as we have a solid cellular signal for our Internet/Wi-Fi. We can survive for two weeks in the boonies with our freshwater and waste tanks, but if we depend on the Internet to make money and pay our bills, going two weeks without a connection is a problem.

"There is no Wi-Fi in the forest, but I promise you will find a better connection."

—Unknown

When we first started talking about the idea of RVing full-time, the very first question we had was, "Can we get sufficient, affordable, reliable Internet to be able to work while we travel?" If we couldn't find that, then it was pointless going any further, as it was a total deal breaker for us. We needed to work to be able to fund our RV lifestyle. Fortunately, with a quick online search, we found "the bible" offering all the answers to our mobile Internet needs: *The Mobile Internet Handbook* (available both as an ebook and in print). The authors update the content frequently in new editions with the most current information. Much like healthcare, connectivity is a fast and ever-changing landscape. With that in mind, we'll make this section a general overview of the basics, and we'll share some resources for you to do some further research.

You might have high-speed cable Internet at your home and place of work, and only use cellular or Wi-Fi data on occasion. In the RV lifestyle your cellular data use is likely to be significantly higher. If you are trying to keep your expenses down, you might use free public Wi-Fi at stores and campgrounds, but those connections are usually less secure and less reliable than we have found our cellular connection to be. You may also be surprised by just how connected you can be when you feel like you are in the middle of nowhere. Let's take a look at your best options for staying connected, with the first two being the most common among full-time RVers:

1. **Cellular Wi-Fi**—available through your cellular provider, usually on your smartphone personal hotspot and/or a personal MiFi or Jetpack

2. **Public Wi-Fi**—available through RV parks and campgrounds, libraries, and some coffee shops, shopping centers, and malls

3. **Cable/DSL**—usually recommended only for those spending longer periods of time, such as a season, at a campsite

4. **Satellite**—not usually needed or recommended, unless you're going waaaay out there (and even then it will be expensive)

As we mentioned, the first two options—cellular and public Wi-Fi—are going to satisfy the needs of most RVers, so let's talk a bit more about those.

CELLULAR WI-FI

You will get the best, most reliable coverage when traveling around the US with a cellular plan from one of the three major US carriers—Verizon, AT&T, and T-Mobile (which is also great for traveling to Canada and Mexico). Smaller carriers, like Sprint, are usually reliable only when spending time around major cities. One of these may work as a backup, but it will be limiting as your only carrier. Verizon and AT&T are the two strongest, with T-Mobile quickly catching up. We currently have all three to ensure that we are always connected, but you won't necessarily need more than one.

Contact your existing cellular and home Internet providers to establish your monthly data usage as a starting point for how much data you may need on the road. You can't get true unlimited cellular data on the road as easily or affordably as you can with home Internet, so you'll need to be more mindful of your data consumption to keep your bills down. That means you may need to curb your addiction to online video streaming and turn off the iCloud sharing feature on your smartphone, especially if you take lots of photos and video, as that syncs to all devices and will eat up your data in no time.

PERSONAL HOTSPOTS VERSUS MIFIS AND JETPACKS

Your Internet setup is going to be an entirely personal decision, based on your needs and budget, but know that many high-tech RVers and digital nomads—including high-level IT professionals and network administrators—live and work full-time from their RVs while traveling the country, and they have found a solution that works for them.

Many RVers with fairly simple online needs—say, checking email, doing online research, and watching a few short-er videos (no heavy streaming)—get by just fine with their smartphone's personal hotspot feature and a cellular data plan with 6–10 GB per month and careful usage.

But for those of us who work full-time or run a business from the road, a separate dedicated MiFi or Jetpack (which you can get from your cellular provider) is a good idea. These are small, portable devices that use your cellular data plan to create a private local Wi-Fi network, and typically allow you to connect five to fifteen devices. Look for an affordable "unlimited" data plan from one of the major carriers. Their plans and offers are always changing, and sometimes you can pick up a good deal. It's important to note that the so-called unlimited data plans are not truly un-limited like your home Internet may be. Unlimited cellular plans come with limitations and may deprioritize or throttle (slow down) your connectivity speeds after reaching a certain amount of data usage until your billing cycle rolls over, or charge for any data overage. Read the fine print before signing a contract so you know what you are truly getting.

"Can you get online everywhere, reliably, with high speeds, and for cheap? Probably not. But being online nearly everywhere and most of the time for an affordable price is within reach."

—Cherie Ve Ard and Chris Dunphy of Technomadia

You may need to plan your travels around where your cellular provider has a reliable signal, but we have been pleasantly surprised by how consistently we have been able to get strong signal on the road. If you have a strong 4G LTE signal, your Internet speeds can be extremely high, even higher than you might experience with your home Internet in some areas. Cellular connectivity and speeds can also vary significantly based on temporary load on the cell tower. You might have a strong signal, but if too many people are using that tower—say, at a major event or holiday that brings a higher than usual number of people to the area—your speeds will suffer, especially if you have a cellular plan with "deprioritization."

Other devices you may want to consider to improve your connectivity are a cellular booster (which uses an antenna to help boost your cellular signal), and a Wi-Fi extender (which allows you to use nearby public Wi-Fi networks more easily).

WHAT ABOUT FREE CAMPGROUND AND PUBLIC WI-FI?

Some campgrounds and RV parks may promote their free Wi-Fi as a perk, but don't plan on it being reliable, secure, or fast enough for your needs, especially if your work depends on it. The same goes for other places with public Wi-Fi that you may be planning to use, such as libraries, coffee shops, shopping malls, breweries, and chain stores. While free campground and public Wi-Fi may be fine for quick Internet searches, checking email, or posting to social media, you will find that service varies everywhere you go, and it's definitely not recommended that you use these for secure things involving sensitive data, like doing your online banking.

RECOMMENDED RESOURCES

As mobile Internet and cellular plans are an ever-changing landscape, we look to mobile Internet and technology experts to keep up with the latest. The best resources we have found include RVMobileInternet.com, run by Chris and Cherie of *Technomadia* (see their case study in this chapter). They offer a free *Facebook* page as well as a paid membership, in which they do all the research for you for between $1 and $2 per week. Their service has saved us thousands of dollars in connectivity fees since joining in 2014, as it helps us stay on top of the latest plans and ensure that we always have the best solution for our needs. We also recommend the blog and *YouTube* videos by digital nomads and tech entrepreneurs Erik and Kala (their case study is featured in Chapter 9), which you can find at LivinLite.net.

You can find more resources, including the gear we use to stay connected, plus nontraditional ways to access "true unlimited" Internet, at our website https://rvlove.com/book-bonus-content.

Peter, 52, and John, 49

FULL-TIME RVERS SINCE APRIL 2003

Website: www.thervgeeks.com

YouTube: RVgeeks

Instagram: @rvgeeks

"Having the freedom to position ourselves in whatever geographic, environmental, social, political, or work setting that brings us happiness and peace of mind is priceless."

FACING CANCER, THEN LOSING A SIBLING, BOTH AT A YOUNG age, brings a certain clarity. This one-and-only, short life we're given can either be lived fully...or not. We realized that living in a certain place and in a certain way, simply due to expectations, both external and self-imposed, was squandering that life.

We fearlessly (or foolishly?) quit our secure corporate jobs and bought an RV, despite never having been in one before. We sold everything we owned and drove away from it all for good. We planned to live off our modest savings for two or three years with little safety net beyond our confidence in ourselves, expecting to fall in love with some special place where the grass was greener than the lawn we left behind. Instead, we fell in love with the freedom to come and go as we please, and can't imagine tying ourselves to a single location again.

After realizing that the "special place" we'd been looking for was everywhere, we had to regroup to continue the journey. Unlike many working-age full-time RVers, we hadn't become nomads with the intention of working along the way. We needed to reevaluate our skill sets if we were to have any chance of staying afloat financially.

We took inventory of every skill, talent, and interest that either one of us felt we possessed, whether utilized professionally in the past or not. When "RVing" was added to our list of marketing, sales, computers, writing, and photography, the math added up to "RV Park Website Designers" and suddenly RVgeeks Website Design was born.

The other half of the equation is keeping costs down. With a modicum of discipline, RVing can be a very economical way to live. But those "sacrifices" became a fun challenge...a game to see how inexpensively we could live. We understood that freedom for us required living within our means.

At about the time we'd achieved some success as website designers, we created several tutorial videos to help some friends learn how to operate their RV. That casual foray into videography blossomed into one of the most popular channels about RVing on *YouTube*. We're grateful and proud of the fact that both our websites and videos have been well received. But we've worked hard to get there, making sure that our integrity and the quality of our work provides value for our customers and viewers alike.

Our freedom comes from our ability to support ourselves in a somewhat unconventional way. We're not all about money, and an honest living is all we require to live this fairly modest nomadic life of ours. Before we started building websites, we always said we'd take on any kind of work to keep RVing. We do, however, feel fortunate to have created a way to support ourselves without resorting to fixed hourly work.

We're as much in love with RVing as ever, and the final chapter of our nomadic story is far from being written.

BALANCING WORK, LIFE, AND TRAVEL

Remember that full-time RVing is a lifestyle, not a vacation. You will be tempted to go faster and to see and explore more when you start out; we all do it, and this is natural for the first few months to a year. But if you want to succeed on the road in the longer term, you need to find a balance or a groove that is sustainable—personally, professionally, and financially.

Come back again to your "why": your reason for doing this. Is it to travel and explore, or to create your own path to freedom by building a new business of your own? Is it to maximize your limited vacation time from work so you're able to more easily explore in the evenings and on weekends?

Are you disciplined enough to focus and work when you need to, even when there are so many cool things on your doorstep? Are you able to set healthy boundaries with your employer—or yourself—when it comes to finding the balance between work and personal downtime? Or are you taking unhealthy work habits on the road? There's a difference between having a strong work ethic and being driven by passion and purpose, and being a workaholic who doesn't know how or when to switch off and unplug.

Suggestions for Balancing Work, Life, and Travel

If you end up consistently working seventy-hour weeks with little time for unplugging and exploring, you may feel that you have traded little more than the size of your home. On the other hand, you may find the temptation of the amazing places you visit hard to resist, and end up not working enough to fulfill your work responsibilities or your income stream. Here are some ways to avoid these pitfalls:

☐ Create a dedicated work or office space in your RV so you can work productively, ideally without impeding on the living space.

☐ Create a work schedule with set hours to provide you with structure. If you're working for a company, share those hours with them.

☐ Set healthy boundaries between work and playtime. If you're tempted to work outside your scheduled time, ask yourself, does that email or phone call really need to be answered tonight? Most likely it's not actually urgent and can be handled the next day during your regularly scheduled hours.

- [ ] Take a walk around the campground or local area before and after your working day to create a separation or "commute" between work and home time.

- [ ] Avoid feeling like you have to work more to prove you're working because you're a remote employee. Some people feel the need to overcompensate for their arrangement by working more often than they should.

- [ ] Slow down your travels and stay longer in an area to improve productivity and focus, and also allow time to see the area before moving on.

- [ ] Camp in more remote or rural areas when you have a lot of work to do, so you'll have fewer distractions and will be less tempted by people to visit and things to do.

- [ ] Aim to have at least one technology-free day per week or month, to really unplug and recharge.

CHAPTER 8

LEGALLY SPEAKING

Domicile, Mail, Voting, Banking, and Taxes

"The path in front of you is rarely a straight line. It's full of bumps, twists, and turns. Embrace the bumps in the road. They are the road."

—Ellen Bennett (a.k.a. the Apron Lady), American entrepreneur and chef

As you move toward your RVing life, you may be wondering about some basic logistical items—how to get your mail, and what address to use for things like your driver's license, taxes, and bank accounts. Then there's how to vote, pay your bills, and handle your banking. If you are maintaining a home and RVing part-time or taking extended trips, it's likely that you will keep your home base. But if you plan to RV full-time, you will have many practical decisions to make around which state you will call home. The decisions regarding your full-time RV life are multifaceted, and you'll need to weigh the pros and cons of everything when narrowing down to what will work best for you. In this chapter we'll walk you through the most important things you need to know so you can feel confident that you are making sound decisions that will support your legal, financial, and personal needs on the road.

CHOOSING YOUR STATE OF DOMICILE

One of the biggest decisions you'll make when deciding to pick up your roots and adopt a mobile lifestyle is choosing which state you will actually call home. You'll often hear RVers joke that "home is where you park it" or "home is where you hook up," and even though you may consider yourself a full-time traveling nomad, for legal purposes you will still need to claim a physical location as "home." Many businesses, and of course, the government, will require you to have a legal, physical address for things like your driver's license, taxes, and bank accounts, to name a few.

RV TERMS TO KNOW

domicile: According to *Black's Law Dictionary*, "a person's domicile is the place where he lives or has his home. In a strict and legal sense, that is properly the domicile of a person where he has his true, fixed, permanent home and principal establishment, and to which, whenever he is absent, he has the intention of returning." Simply put, for RVers it is the place (state, city, address) you choose as your home, especially for legal and tax purposes.

residence: This is where you reside, usually your home. It means living in a particular locality and simply requires bodily presence as an inhabitant in a given place. You can have more than one residence, but only one residence can be nominated as your domicile.

You may not have heard the term *domicile* before, as it's not something people usually talk about in their regular lives. For most people, their primary home or residence is also their domicile, as they are usually one and the same. But for people who have more than one home in different parts of the country or world, the one they choose as their primary residence will be considered their domicile. As an RVer, your home is traveling with you. In the winter it might be by the beach in Florida, and in the summer it might be situated among the mountains in Colorado. So, where do you truly live?

Domicile is defined as where you consider home to be, or where you plan to return to after your travels. A residence is where you live temporarily. You can have as many residences as you like, but you can have only one domicile. You might hit the road with the intention of finding a new place to call home and put down roots again. But while you are figuring that out, you will still need to claim one location as your domicile.

FACTORS TO THINK ABOUT

You might choose to continue to claim the city and state you departed from as your domicile. Maybe you have family or friends in the area who are okay with you using their address as your own, as though you are staying in a spare room or sleeping on their couch long term. However, if you are looking for a more permanent domicile solution, this can be a much more complicated question, as there are many factors to consider when choosing your optimal domicile. Domicile is a highly personal choice, and only you will know enough about your situation to know what is right for you. Detailed analysis of each variable is beyond the scope of this book, let alone this chapter, and we are not legal experts on the important subject of domicile, but the information we share in this chapter will help guide your thinking and let you know where you need to do more research, allowing you to make an informed and confident decision. You may also choose to get legal advice to assist you in this matter.

If you are looking to make a change, Florida, South Dakota, and Texas are all good places for you to start your research, as these states are RVer-friendly, making it easier to handle many things (like vehicle registration) for those of us living a mobile life. The other advantage of setting up your new "home" in an RV-friendly state is that with so many other RVers also claiming it as home, the RVers and organizations become very influential when it comes to local laws. In some areas there are more RVers registered as voters than there are people who physically reside there. Escapees RV Club, in particular, is very strong in providing advocacy for RVers, as they have so many members, a significant percentage of whom are full-time RVers, which makes for a very large "population" in the town where they are headquartered.

Where Should Your Domicile Be?

Here is a list of considerations that might affect your domicile choice:

- The length of time you plan on RVing
- Whether or not you plan to sell your traditional home
- The location of your employer or place of business
- Tax laws relating to real estate, pensions, sales, income, wills, estates, investments, etc.
- Health insurance availability and pricing
- Vehicle insurance, inspection, and registration requirements
- Voting and jury duty eligibility

- Community involvement and/or political environment
- Laws around contracts, partnerships, corporations, or marriages
- Laws related to possessions, permitting, and medical treatments
- Education tuition for you or your children
- Licensing requirements for large vehicles
- Ease of working with a state or local government when out of state
- Weather conditions during the time of year when you might need to visit
- The total time you plan to spend in a state or county per year
- How many family members and friends live there
- Your interest in returning to the area when not traveling

Of course, the simpler your life is before your transition to RV life, the easier the decisions are. The amount of research required is directly related to how many of the previously listed variables affect you, and doing your research can allow you to maximize the benefits for your individual circumstances. This chapter will explain some of these topics in greater detail to give you more perspective on their impact, starting with taxes.

TAXES: SALES, INCOME, AND PROPERTY

Every government needs to generate revenue one way or another. Some states focus on doing that through property tax or income tax, while others might focus on sales tax. If you are looking to purchase a $300,000 motorhome, you might be drawn to a state that charges no sales tax, when others charge over 8 percent. That alone could mean a savings of $24,000 in sales tax. On the other hand, if you plan to spend only $30,000 on your RV, and your income is $100,000 per year, you might be more interested in a state that has lower income tax versus sales tax. California income tax rates are as high as 13 percent, while some other states, like Texas, Florida, South Dakota, Nevada, Washington, Wyoming, and Alaska, have no state income tax.

Perhaps you are approaching or are already at retirement age and have income from social security, investments, dividends, rental properties, or a military or other pension. Maybe you have a large nest egg that you plan to leave to your children and are mindful of inheritance taxes. Tax rules and rates will vary for all of those different revenue streams depending on your chosen domicile, so this decision can get pretty complicated.

Property-related taxes can be important too. If you don't own property, you don't need to pay property tax, but if you DO own property in a state with high property tax, you may find that your RV loan payment ends up being less than what you used to pay on property tax alone. If you currently own property and are planning on selling that property to venture into full-time RV life, be very careful about changing your domicile before you sell and close on that property. Some states—Maryland and Rhode Island are two examples—currently have a property-related tax that very few know about, including some realtors. This special tax comes into effect only if you are selling a property and are not currently domiciled in that same state. The tax in Maryland is 7.5 percent of the total transaction price, so if you sold a $400,000 home, you could get hit with a $30,000 bill that you could have avoided by simply keeping your driver's license and domicile in Maryland until after the sale of your property closed. Sometimes it makes sense to change your domicile before you hit the road but not always, so do your research.

OTHER FACTORS: INSURANCE, EDUCATION, EASE, AND ETHICS

Once you figure out which state has the most favorable tax environment for you, look at other important factors that may sway your decision about domicile, even though their financial impact may be lower.

INSURANCE

Insurance is a big factor as, similar to taxes, there are several types of insurance. Health insurance pricing and availability, which we covered in Chapter 6, can have an enormous impact on domicile decisions. We have known several RVers who changed their state of domicile solely based on health insurance needs. Many states do not support national insurance coverage, which can be a deal breaker for some full-time RVers who travel all around the country. The rules and regulations around health insurance continue to change often and fast, so again, this is something you'll need to keep a regular eye on in case things change in a way that affects you.

Vehicle insurance rates also vary across the country, and if you have a less than stellar driving record or a history of insurance claims, this could add up to large swings in the cost of insuring your RV. Insurance rates are based on historical data and can change at any time, but at the time of writing, Ohio had the lowest and Florida had the highest vehicle insurance rates. The rates in Florida can be as much as four times higher than those in Ohio. This may not be enough to outweigh other considerations, but it is definitely a factor to consider in the big picture.

Robert, 56, and
Veronica, 56

WE BOUGHT OUR RV IN 2015 AND LIVED IN
IT PART-TIME UNTIL WE SOLD OUR HOUSE AND
STARTED RVING FULL-TIME IN AUGUST 2016.

"RVing offers us the
ability to truly experience
a location longer and
more in depth than
a typical vacation would."

WE HAVE FAMILY SCATTERED UP AND DOWN THE EASTERN HALF of the country and also some on the West Coast. We got tired of flying everywhere and staying in hotels and guest rooms, so we started thinking that bringing our own home with us might be a good idea.

We sold our home after realizing we were paying for a four-bedroom house in one of the most expensive areas of the country, but only spending about two months of the year in it. The hardest part of selling the house was ruthlessly paring down what we wanted to keep in storage. After that, we hired an estate liquidation company and a wholesaler to completely empty out the house. We were able to empty everything and close on our home sale in less than eight weeks!

We often get asked how much it costs to be a full-timer, but the cost of an RVer's lifestyle is completely driven by each individual. We sold a house that cost a lot to maintain, especially when you consider New Jersey property and income taxes. We also balance out the cost of campgrounds; our most expensive are in the Florida Keys in the winter and Myrtle Beach in the summer. The rest of the time we stay at places that are much less costly. We balance our time in the RV with other trips. We have been to Mexico, Canada, the Caribbean, China, Europe, England, Ireland, and Scotland, mostly paid for

with travel points. When we changed our domicile and residence to Florida, we took the money we saved on taxes and started applying it to our RV loan, allowing us to stay ahead of the depreciation of the RV. We waited until we sold our house before changing domicile to avoid legal issues and tax penalties. We changed to Florida because it is the state we spend the most time in. Luckily, Florida also happens to not have state income taxes! We use the Good Sam Club mail-forwarding service, which has been fine. We did run into an issue with a credit card company that maintained that using a mail-forwarding service as our permanent address violates the Patriot Act; however, they seem to accept it now. We immediately got our driver's licenses, registered our vehicles, and registered to vote.

It is our choice what to make of the time we have left in our lives. After thinking about what we wanted to do with our lives, we decided we wanted to spend it visiting our parents, family, and friends, who were spread all across the US and in other countries around the world. The RV lifestyle has enabled us to travel the way we like, spend time with our loved ones, and be comfortable at the same time. Not having the house and being careful in our spending have enabled us to have a lifestyle that we once only dreamed about.

Some other factors to consider might include:

- Will you need to return to the state for vehicle registration and inspections?

- If so, when will you need to return, and how will that affect your travels?

- Does the state require any special licenses to drive larger vehicles?

- California requires a special driver's license if your RV is more than 40 feet in length.

- Texas requires one if your RV exceeds a certain weight (e.g., if you're towing more than 10,000 pounds or driving an RV that weighs more than 26,000 pounds).

- Other states allow you to drive into a dealership in a compact car and drive off in a 45-foot-long motorhome weighing over 40,000 pounds—on the same driver's license!

- Having the correct class of driver's license is important, not only to comply with the laws of your domicile state, and to avoid a ticket in case you are pulled over by law enforcement, but also in the event of an insurance claim, to help avoid the risk of being denied.

EDUCATION

If you plan on traveling with school-age children, it is important to know that homeschooling is legal throughout America but rules vary significantly from state to state. You can learn more about the legalities and requirements of homeschooling on websites like https://hslda.org and www.responsiblehomeschooling.org.

If you are paying for college tuition—your own or your kids'—domicile may impact your eligibility for tuition at the educational institution of your choice. If you're hitting the road with kids, especially teenagers, you will want to look ahead a few years and think about where they might prefer to go to college, and consider the domicile requirements that will allow them to attend an in-state college or university, to avoid paying the higher rates of out-of-state tuition.

EASE

Many other laws and policies can make it easier or more difficult to deal with a chosen city, county, or state, and all of these should be considered in your decision. For example, we are domiciled out of a county in Texas that allows us to change our vehicle license plates and renew annual registrations via mail, which is extremely convenient. However, our friends Charles and Abby are currently domiciled in Arizona and drive a 2010 motorhome that they purchased in August 2016. Due to the age and purchase month of their RV, they have to return to Arizona in the heat of summer for an emissions test and to renew their RV registration each year. This limits their travel flexibility, so they decided to change their domicile to Florida, which has no emissions testing and allows them to renew their annual registration by mail.

ETHICS

There is another aspect of the decision that may end up being the most important of all for you, and that is the ethical consideration. One of the critical pieces related to choosing a new domicile is being comfortable calling the new state "home." Do you feel that you could comfortably connect and blend with the environment? By this we mean not just the landscape and weather, but also the social, political, legal, and economic environment.

"You don't have to live your life the way other people expect you to."

—*Chris Guillebeau, American author*

Perhaps you have very deep family roots in an area, and though you like the idea of traveling for a bit, you know deep down that you will always plan to return. On the other hand, maybe all you know for now is that you want to explore, and although you don't know where you will eventually land, it won't be where you left from. In this case, you'll just be looking for the domicile that will be most supportive of your current lifestyle and easiest to deal with, and that will offer the most benefits in the specific areas that are most important for your needs.

Keep in mind that your previous domicile state might not like the loss in tax revenue resulting from you leaving and, in some cases, could dispute your claim of changed domicile. Some states, like Minnesota and California, are more tax aggressive and have reputations for challenging domicile changes, so if you decide to change, make sure you cover all your bases.

WHAT'S INVOLVED IN CHANGING DOMICILE?

The main task ahead of you when changing domicile as an RVer is establishing intent. You need to show evidence of your intent to leave the state you are from, and establish a strong connection to the state you are changing domicile to. Subsequently, your intent is really broken down into two main pieces: a paper trail and establishing a connection to a new community.

THE PAPER TRAIL

You will want to have physical evidence of your new address showing up on important paperwork and identification documents. You will need to change your driver's license, insurances, bank statements, tax records, investments, employer records, legal documents, voting registration, cell phone bills, health providers—anything and everything that was formerly mailed to your old address should be changed to your new address. You can't keep a foot in two camps. It is very important that you use one domicile for everything. The last thing you want is to be carrying conflicting information on your documents.

CONNECTING WITH A NEW COMMUNITY

The second element of intent is establishing a connection with your new community. This can be a bit more challenging, especially as you'll be traveling so much, but it is still an important aspect. Ways to establish community connections include:

- Establishing relationships with doctors, lawyers, accountants, financial advisers, or other professional offices in your new state
- Moving your things to a storage unit in your new domicile state and county (that is, if you are storing anything)
- Visiting or joining local branches of a club or organization you belong to

If you decide to make a change, make it fully, for a clean break and to safeguard yourself.

WHAT ABOUT VOTING AND JURY DUTY?

You'll want to consider your options and related rules and regulations around voting when selecting your state of domicile. If you select one of the RV-friendly states as your legal domicile, you will be able to vote simply by receiving a ballot in the mail, then marking your choices and mailing it back. You can do your research on the ballot issues in advance, and you don't have to find a polling location or wait in line. Just be sure to request a mail-in ballot well in advance to allow time for mail forwarding and sending it back by the due date.

Similarly, if you choose an RV-friendly county and state, they will be more willing to work with you in the event that you receive a jury summons. If you receive a summons when you are out of state, they will be lenient in excusing you from the responsibility and/or allow you to reschedule for a time when you intend to be back in the area.

HOW DO YOU GET YOUR MAIL?

This is one of the first questions we're usually asked about our full-time RV life, and it may be a big question for you too. In this day and age, even though we handle so much correspondence online, we all still get sent physical, printed snail mail—whether we like it or not—and we have to find a way to receive it, even when we're constantly on the move.

When you are first starting out as an RVer, you may decide to simply have your mail forwarded to a local family member (as we did for the first six months) or trusted friend, or even hire a personal assistant and have them forward your mail every so often when you arrive at a campground or location. This works for many RVers in the short term, and it can even work for some for many years. Of course, we're presuming here that you will have already digitized as much of your life as possible to reduce the amount of time-sensitive physical mail that you receive.

Many RVers choose to have their mail handled by one of the many professional mail-forwarding companies that can be found in many states, including the three most popular states for full-time RVers—Florida, South Dakota, and Texas. Many of these mail-forwarding companies are part of larger RV-focused organizations, like Escapees and FMCA, which can also support you in changing your state of domicile. Some popular mail-forwarding services among full-time RVers and travelers include America's Mailbox, Escapees Mail Service, FMCA Mail Service, Good Sam Mail Service, and St. Brendan's Isle. For more useful information on mail-forwarding services, please visit https://rvlove.com/book-bonus-content.

WHAT DOES A MAIL-FORWARDING SERVICE DO?

On a basic level a mail-forwarding service will:

- Provide you with an address to use while traveling
- Hold and manage your mail
- Forward mail on to you at a time and place that is convenient to you—usually when you get settled into an RV park or campground

Your mail-forwarding company will provide you with a unique address that will usually include a unit number, or "apartment" number, that can serve as a permanent address for most of your other legal documents, bills, and paperwork. Your mail (and packages, if you wish) will be delivered to the centralized location and sorted into your individual box. Part of setting up your account is establishing rules about what type of mail you want to receive and forward, as there's no point in paying good money to forward junk mail—unless you really want it! (In fact, we like the "no junk mail" option of our mail-forwarding company so much that we would likely continue using their service even if we chose to return to a stick-and-brick home, especially as we don't intend to ever stop traveling completely.)

A mail-forwarding service can do many other things too. Here is a list of potential features, services, and additional considerations that may help you determine which mail-forwarding service is the best fit for you.

❏ Physical sorting of mail
❏ Separating first class mail from "junk" mail
❏ Scanning mail pieces for online viewing
❏ Opening mail and scanning contents of envelopes for online viewing
❏ Reading mail to you when you call

As you decide which service or package is right for you, think about these considerations:

❏ Can it handle parcels and larger packages?
❏ Do you need to be a member of the organization to use the service?

- ☐ What are the hours/days of availability?
- ☐ Is it staffed to promptly service your needs?
- ☐ Do you trust the company/organization to handle your more sensitive documents?
- ☐ What is the longevity and stability of the company (i.e., will they be there as long as you need them)?
- ☐ Are their services available in the state that you claim for your domicile?
- ☐ Can the address function as a residential/domicile address, not just for mail?
- ☐ Can they provide assistance and guidance for establishing domicile, registering vehicles, etc.?

ARRANGING MAIL FORWARDING

When you arrive in a location where you are ready to receive your mail, you will contact your mail-forwarding company (usually by phone, email, or online) with your forwarding address, and they will send your mail to you wherever you specify. And since they have presorted your mail, you only pay the postage to receive the mail you actually want.

Keep in mind that not all RV parks and campgrounds will accept mail or packages for you. And if you mostly boondock in the middle of free public lands, there likely won't be a building in sight, let alone a mailbox. In that case, you can simply have your mail-forwarding company send your mail to "General Delivery" at the local post office, clearly marked with your name, of course. Post offices usually hold General Delivery mail for up to fourteen days before returning to sender, so you don't need to be precise on arrival dates. We have learned from experience that it's usually better to wait until we arrive at our destination before arranging mail forwarding, as travel plans can—and often do—change unexpectedly.

Here's an example of how you should address your mail when it's being forwarded to General Delivery at a local USPS post office, with your name, city, state, and zip code:

Marc and Julie Bennett
% GENERAL DELIVERY
Thousand Palms, CA 92276

Not all post offices accept General Delivery mail and packages, so it's best to check first by calling them, doing a quick online search, or asking someone at the local RV park or campground to advise you.

"There are so many special people to meet, so many beautiful places to see, and so many adventures to take! And you're never too old to do any of it!"

Michael, 75, and Daryl (Dee), 70

FULL-TIME RVERS SINCE JULY 2010

Website: http://gonerving.blogspot.com

Facebook: GoneRVing

RVillage: GoneRVing

OUR FULL-TIME RV LIFE STARTED WITH US WANTING TO help care for an aging loved one in America while we were living in Canada. The idea was to spend as much time in the US with her as we could, and the rest of the time in Canada with our grown children and grandchildren. We could not afford to do this and maintain a home in Canada, so the home and everything in it was sold or donated. We set off in our 30-foot Class C motorhome in 2010.

We supported our loved one for two years until her passing, traveling back and forth from Canada as needed to meet domicile and residence legal requirements. We changed RVs and travel style a few times over the following seven years of full-timing. We now have a park model in Canada and a smaller trailer to travel in America during the winter.

We spend the summer running around getting in visits to doctors, dentists, and opticians while we are home in Ontario so that we have a clean bill of health when we cross into the US. Legally, we have to be in Ontario only five months of the year to maintain our free healthcare through the Ontario government. We purchase shorter-term travel insurance for when we are south of the border.

Our address is our daughter's home in Ontario, and she sends our mail to us about once a month. I am usually able to predict where we will be for her to send the package of mail.

We are allowed to stay in America only up to 182 days a year, to prove that we have a closer connection to Canada than the US, and that we are not taking jobs from US citizens. Without special documentation (we have to submit a Form 8840, Closer Connection Exception Statement for Aliens, to the Treasury Department each year) we would be allowed to stay in the United States for only 120 days per year. We also take out catastrophic travel insurance with a high deductible to cover us in the event that we need medical treatment during our time in the US. We find a lot of good information for Canadian snowbirds at www.snowbirdadvisor.ca.

We travel thousands of miles every year, sometimes going hundreds of miles out of our way to meet up with other RVer friends.

The result of our lifestyle choice is that we are healthier, happier, and having a wonderful time meeting some of the most generous, fantastic people ever.

If you are able to receive mail or packages at an RV park or campground, have your mail and packages addressed like this example, showing the full address and your RV site number, if possible, to ensure it gets to you safely:

Marc and Julie Bennett—RV Site 111

Awesome RV Resort

123 Freedom Street

Surprise, AZ 85335

DEALING WITH TIME-SENSITIVE MAIL

Of course, waiting to have your mail forwarded will cause delays in receiving your mail. It isn't very often that you receive physical mail that is extremely time-sensitive these days, but bills from driving toll roads can be a good example, as they will scan your license plate and then send an invoice, which usually needs to be paid within a couple of weeks.

If you are expecting something important or time-sensitive, you can request that the sender send it to you directly, via USPS Priority Mail or an express carrier to your current location, instead of via your mail-forwarding center. However, that's not always possible, especially with legal or financial documents, which may have to be sent directly to the address shown in their records.

RECEIVING PACKAGES

Most mail-forwarding companies will also accept and forward packages for you, but if you are shopping online, it will usually make more sense to have packages shipped directly to your current location so you get them faster and avoid paying double shipping costs.

Before sending any mail, placing orders, or shipping any packages be sure to check with the RV park, campground, or post office to be certain that you are able to receive it. Some private RV parks and campgrounds (not national, state, or city parks) allow USPS, FedEx, UPS, and other carriers to deliver directly to your campsite, and sometimes they will accept deliveries at the Welcome Center/Ranger Station for you to collect. Some RV parks may charge a fee for this. Always ask, as the rules and policies around mail and packages vary everywhere you go.

Having your mail or packages sent to local UPS or FedEx stores is also a handy option. However, they usually charge a fee for this—typically around $5 each—so try to consolidate mail and packages as much as you can.

Like many RVers, we do a lot of shopping on Amazon Prime because it's more convenient and we can get fast delivery (usually within two days, sometimes the next day). RVers tend to do a lot of our shopping online because we often find ourselves in smaller towns that don't necessarily have the stores that carry the item we are looking for, or it may just not be as convenient to drive around in unfamiliar areas looking for supplies. Of course, there are usually big chains in just about every sizable town, so a familiar national store is never far away.

HOW MUCH DOES A MAIL-FORWARDING SERVICE COST?

Depending on the company you choose, mail-forwarding services typically range from about $8 to $30 a month, depending on the level of service you choose, plus actual postage and mail-forwarding costs.

We consider the cost of our mail-forwarding service to be very reasonable and affordable for the services provided. In fact, we now pay less for the service than we used to pay a family member in Amazon gift cards to say "thanks for handling our mail" during our first six months on the road. Our mail company is well staffed to handle our inquiries, we know our mail is in a safe location, we're not inconveniencing anyone, and we're happy to pay for such an invaluable service that makes our life on the road so much easier.

BANKING AND CREDIT CARDS

If you are already doing most of your banking online, you may not have to make too many changes when it comes to your banking, but there are still a few things you'll want to consider as you transition to full-time RV life. If, however, you're used to going into the local branch of your bank or credit union, now's as good a time as any to start getting familiar with taking your banking online, or you may need to consider changing to a bank with a national branch network.

Local banks and credit unions have their merits, but when you plan to travel extensively, choosing a credit union that is part of a national network or a bank that has a national presence will quickly become valuable. We find that it is rare that we need to visit a physical location for our banking needs, but when we do, belonging to a national bank usually means that there is a branch in every major city, and even many small towns.

Finding a Bank That Works for Your RV Life

There are many features to consider when choosing a bank. Here is a list of things to consider as you get started:

☐ Size of ATM network

☐ Number of banks in their network, and locations (some may still only be regional)

☐ Ability to deposit checks online

☐ Limits on size of withdrawal or deposits

☐ Ability to send wire transfers or other digital payments

☐ Credit card offerings

☐ Ability to view credit card and bank statements, and make payments, online

☐ Availability and functionality of a smartphone app

☐ Ability to make cash withdrawals when making purchases at grocery stores

☐ Fees related to ATM and foreign transactions

☐ Required minimum balance or number of transactions to avoid fees

CREDIT CARDS

We would also recommend having multiple credit cards and banking accounts because credit cards and banks occasionally lock up accounts if security gets compromised, rendering the card or bank account unavailable for a period of time. (Yes, this happens even when you call the banks and credit card companies and they put notes in your files that you travel extensively and regularly.) Having an alternate card or bank can keep things running smoothly for you.

Though we have met many RVers who like to avoid using credit cards for a variety of reasons, and we agree that if you are not careful with cards, you can find yourself in financial trouble quickly, we really value the use of our credit cards and make the most of them. We are extremely disciplined about paying them off in full every month to avoid paying the exorbitant interest fees. We love the convenience of ordering online, and also enjoy credit cards that allow you to collect points; in fact, the points we earn heavily subsidize our travel expenses outside of our RV. Many credit cards that offer points give incentives for types of spending that can provide two to five times the number of points for a transaction. By maximizing these benefits we have been able to accumulate enough points to cover the cost of airfares, hotels, and rental cars on multiple trips away from the RV. To learn more about how to maximize using points

for travel, we recommend NomadicMatt.com and also ThePointsGuy.com. Credit cards, when used properly, can also provide additional consumer protections and insurances. There are a whole host of benefits if you are disciplined and research how to optimize them.

PAYING TAXES

Taxes have the potential to get complicated, depending on your sources of income and how you report it. We are not providing professional legal, financial, or tax advice anywhere in this book, only sharing our experiences, and we recommend that you seek professional advice for your personal needs.

That said, from what we have seen out on the road, most people receive money from employers, businesses, or investments at their bank in their domicile state, and are not necessarily generating that income in other states, which then could mean that they file taxes only for that state. Others generate specific income based on specific transactions that are based, or occur, in the state they are residing in, regardless of domicile. If that occurs in a tax-aggressive state, they might come looking for their fair share of the tax revenue. For example, if you are domiciled in an income tax–free state, like Texas, but you spend significant time in California and are regularly conducting business with Californian businesses that are paying you directly and then file their taxes reporting the income they paid you, there is a chance that California will be wondering why they didn't see income tax from you. Especially if you are originally from California and used to pay California income tax, they may chase you down to demand their share.

As mentioned, this topic can be very complicated and is way too individualized for the scope of this book, but we wanted to at least call your attention to the fact that depending on your revenue sources, you may need to file state taxes in multiple states.

Federal tax submittals will be relatively unchanged by your chosen state of domicile, but state taxes can vary significantly. Further, if you normally donate to charitable organizations in your local area or state, and then change domicile, you may want to find similar charities in your new chosen domicile to donate to, thus breaking ties with your former state, and take steps to establish ties to your new state.

Whew! Yes, there are lots of logistical elements, but don't let them scare you. It really is not as overwhelming as it might first appear. Many of these issues are ones that you'll research, decide upon, and then just maintain.

CHAPTER 9

TRAVEL DESTINATIONS AND TRIP PLANNING

Let the Adventures Begin

"I haven't been everywhere, but it's on my list."

—Susan Sontag, American writer, filmmaker, teacher, and political activist

And now, what you've been waiting for: planning your RV travels and adventures! It's been quite the journey, getting through all of the steps of the previous chapters to help you get prepared, set up, and ready to launch into your RV life. Now you're ready to hit the road and see where it takes you. In this chapter we'll cover some trip highlights, as recommended by other full-time RVers, and share options on where you can stay. Whether you're a planner or a non-planner; drive a big rig or a small one; intend to stay in national parks, private RV parks, resorts, and campgrounds or head out deep into nature to camp for free on public lands, or even a Walmart parking lot—we've got you covered.

Plus, there'll be some important things that every RVer needs to be mindful of, like trip and route planning and weather, to keep you safe out there, and we'll go over those too. Finally, we'll share some of the RV and camping clubs that can enhance your experience and save you money along the way, before wrapping up with some ideas for combining RVing with cruising and international travel. What are you waiting for? Let's go!

WHERE DO YOU WANT TO GO?

You have likely already been building a mental list of places you want to visit with your RV, whether you plan to RV for a fixed period of time, part-time, or full-time as a change in lifestyle. You may recall that in Chapter 2 we invited you to define your "why" and list some of the experiences you hope to gain from your RV travels. For some, it may be to immerse in nature and explore our national parks and national monuments. For others, it may be to reconnect with friends and family around the country. Maybe you're a sports lover and want to visit every stadium in the country or follow your favorite team to their games. Or perhaps you're a history buff and want to visit famous historical places, like Gettysburg, firsthand to visualize the amazing events that transpired there, and stand on the same ground as those who changed the course of history. You may wish to visit every state capital or learn from the presidential libraries around the country. You might be ready to drink cocktails in Key West, hike mountains in Colorado, drive coastal roads in Maine, or visit craft breweries in Bend, Oregon. You might want to do a walking food tour around Miami or feel the power and beauty of Niagara Falls, cross the border into Canada or visit the last frontier—Alaska!

"The purpose of life, after all, is to live it, to taste experience to the utmost, to reach out eagerly and without fear for newer and richer experience."

—Eleanor Roosevelt, former first lady of the United States

It may not even matter where you go—you may be more interested in the people you get to see or the things you get to experience. You might choose to focus on simple things, like immersing in nature, spending more time outdoors, breathing in fresh air, hiking more, wiggling your toes in sand on beaches in every corner of the continent, taking a dip in the Atlantic and Pacific Oceans, fishing more, relaxing more, and watching more sunsets.

The list of places to visit and things to see is truly unlimited. Your list is likely going to expand faster than you can check things off, especially as you meet more RVers along the way who will recommend so many other great places you may never have heard of or thought about. Even though we have been traveling full-time since 2014 and have visited all fifty US states, we still feel we have only scratched the surface of all we want to see and do. We're so glad we started when we did, and you will be too.

FINDING INSPIRATION

There are plenty of great books, blogs, *YouTube* channels, and other resources with detailed tips on where to go and what to see and do. Some of our favorite resources include the free Lonely Planet City Guide apps and guidebooks that cover specific regions and road trips, the Roadtrippers website and app, and the Oh, Ranger! ParkFinder app. Or maybe you're the kind of traveler who just likes to see where the road takes you, in which case, you won't need much more than a road atlas, a GPS, or some apps and guidebooks to help you uncover roads less traveled.

PLANNING A ROUTE

Where should you start? Unless you want to haphazardly zigzag across the country (which won't be very efficient in terms of time, miles, or fuel costs), you will likely want to put in at least a little bit of general planning, even if you aren't much of a planner. (That said, if you really do just want to travel completely serendipitously and on a whim, to see where the road takes you, that can be a fun adventure too!) Here are some steps for figuring out your route:

1. Start by writing out a list of all of the places you have heard about and want to see, plus any special events you may want to attend.

2. Write out another list of the people you want to visit and their locations.

3. Mark each location you want to visit on a map. (You might need some help from online searches to identify exactly where all those places are, but it won't take long, and as an RVer, you'll find that your geography skills will improve quickly!)

4. Once you have all the markers on your map, you'll start noticing clusters of markers in the same area. You'll want to put the regions with the highest number of markers high on your priority list.

5. Look at what lies in between where you currently are and where you are headed, to identify any places or adventure items that appear en route to your primary destination regions. Apps like Roadtrippers are a great way to discover attractions or places of interest that you never would have otherwise known about. If you were traveling by air, you might visit only your primary destination and return. But when you are traveling by RV, short diversions while en route to your primary destination are part of what makes a road trip memorable!

MUST-SEE DESTINATIONS IN NORTH AMERICA

- National parks and national monuments. Our national park system is truly incredible! You can make it your mission to see them all, but here are some of our favorites: Yellowstone, Yosemite, Glacier, Redwood, Grand Canyon (South and North Rims), Bryce Canyon, Zion, Capitol Reef, Crater Lake, Badlands, and Rocky Mountain National Parks. Some of our favorite national monuments include Bandelier, Carlsbad Caverns, and White Sands.

- State parks and forests. Reconnect with nature at state parks and forests everywhere.

- Historic Route 66. Fun, quirky, historic, and kitsch.

- Highway 1. Drive the coastal route from Oregon to California and stop at Bixby Bridge near Big Sur, California, to snap an obligatory selfie.

- Oregon Coast lighthouses. Visit, hike, and climb to the top of as many as you can.

- Quartzsite, Arizona. For serenity in the desert visit in November, December, February, or March. Visit in the last two weeks of January and see the place bustling at its peak, with tens of thousands of RVers boondocking in the desert.

- San Francisco, California. Drive over the Golden Gate Bridge and visit the Napa Valley.

- The Rockies. Hike, bike, or go fishing in and around them.

- Sedona, Arizona. Discover vortexes, hike red rock canyons, and explore jeeping trails.

- Savannah, Georgia. Soak up southern charm, history, and natural beauty.

- The Olympic Peninsula, Washington. Explore the diversity of lakes, waterfalls, rivers, mountains, rainforests, and beaches.

- Washington, DC. Visit monuments and museums, including at least one Smithsonian.

- Alaska. For adventure, epic scenery, wildlife, the midnight sun, and salmon runs.

- Canada. In particular Banff, Jasper, and the Icefields Parkway—the Canadian Rockies.

21 THINGS TO DO

1. Hike the Narrows in Zion National Park, Utah.

2. See the fall colors of New England.

3. Go bicycling on Mackinac Island in Michigan (a no-car island accessible only by boat).

4. Do a photographer's tour of Antelope Canyon (slot canyon on Navajo land in Arizona).

5. Visit the Whitney Plantation Museum outside of New Orleans.

6. Swim with manatees in Florida.

7. Go hot air ballooning at the Albuquerque International Balloon Fiesta in New Mexico.

8. Attend a live concert at the Grand Ole Opry in Nashville, Tennessee.

9. Visit Death Valley, Arizona, in spring for the wildflower bloom.

10. People watch during happy hour over sunset cocktails in Key West, Florida.

11. Watch the sunrise from Cadillac Mountain in Acadia National Park, Maine.

12. Visit Louisville, Kentucky, to explore thoroughbred horse country and hit the Kentucky Bourbon Trail.

13. Visit presidential libraries around the country.

14. Experience the Birmingham Civil Rights Institute in Alabama.

15. Attend one of the big RV shows, like Hershey, Pennsylvania, in September or Tampa, Florida, in January.

16. Walk across the border from Yuma, Arizona, into Los Algodones, Mexico, for a teeth cleaning.

17. Snap a photo standing on the corner of Winslow, Arizona.

18. Visit the Henry Ford Museum and Greenfield Village in Dearborn, Michigan.

19. Take a plunge into the chilly volcanic waters of Crater Lake in Oregon.

20. Visit cultural icons like Graceland (in Memphis, Tennessee), the Hollywood Walk of Fame (in Los Angeles, California), and the Prada Marfa store (outside Marfa, Texas).

21. Boondock among the cacti on BLM land in the Southwest desert.

WHEN SHOULD YOU GO?

Something you will definitely want to consider in your travel planning is WHEN to go. Some destinations on your list may be better to visit at certain times of year. You won't want to visit Maine in the winter or Death Valley, California, in the summer, especially in an RV! You also need to consider the elevation of your destination. If you've lived your whole life at or near sea level, you may not fully understand the impact that elevation can have on temperatures. Palm Springs, California, is a perfect example, as the main city is near sea level and is generally nice and warm in the winter, which makes it a popular destination for snowbirds. There are mountains nearby that gain substantial elevation quickly. A couple of years ago, while staying in the Palm Springs area in our RV, we took a dip in the pool in the morning. That same afternoon we took a ten-minute ride in the aerial tram up to Mt. San Jacinto State Park, an elevation of 8,516 feet. While we were hiking to the top of a nearby mountain, it began snowing on us. There was a temperature swing of greater than 30°F from the mountain where we stood to the city of Palm Springs below us.

Generally speaking, most RVers will plan on heading north in the summer and south in the winter to make the most of the optimal weather for travel and enjoying the outdoors. That said, there are plenty of RVers who brave the extreme temperatures for their favorite activities in the hot or cold seasons.

You may also want to attend events that happen on specific dates or during a certain time of year. For example, in January 2017 we decided we wanted to see the total solar eclipse from Madras, Oregon, in August, as NASA claimed Madras was one of the best places in the country to view it. Being such a popular event—and one that happens very rarely—we made our travel plans and reservations eight months in advance, to spend three weeks beforehand at a campground in Bend, before moving to Madras, where we spent five days boondocking in a field with about 20,000 people! Some avid astronomy friends made their Madras plans two years in advance so they could secure a campsite with water and electric hookups. Events like the Albuquerque International Balloon Fiesta are also very popular with RVers in September/October each year, as are campgrounds in the Northeast during the fall colors season, and during winter in Florida. Book in advance if you want to be sure there's a campsite waiting for you; however, there are always people who prefer going with the flow and will arrive without a reservation. Sometimes this works out—there are often last-minute cancellations—and sometimes it doesn't, and then you'll have to be flexible and keep moving along or calling around until you find somewhere that can accommodate you—or find somewhere to dry camp. Ultimately, it's up to you whether you want to plan well in advance or not.

When Making Reservations in Advance Is a Good Idea

- [ ] When you want to be certain you have a campsite confirmed before arrival
- [ ] During peak times in central, northern, and popular areas, generally Memorial Day through Labor Day
- [ ] During peak times in southern areas popular with snowbirds (e.g., Arizona, Florida, Texas, and California), generally November through March
- [ ] During public and major holidays in most popular areas, especially near beaches, lakes, and tourist attractions
- [ ] When you want to camp inside of popular national and state parks, and have certainty around your campsite availability and location
- [ ] If you have a "big rig" that is difficult or more limiting to find campsites for
- [ ] If you have to be in a certain place at a certain time, and don't have flexibility around your dates

The bigger your RV setup, the more planning you'll need to do, and the smaller your RV, the more flexibility you will have and therefore, the easier it will be to find campsites, as you will be able to fit in more spaces. And while bigger RVs are definitely more limiting, especially in many national and state parks, it's not impossible to make it work. You may not be willing to trade a more comfortable living space for the ability to fly by the seat of your pants when it comes to finding campsites for your RV. On the other hand, you may place a higher value on flexibility and increased accessibility in your travels, and therefore be more willing to go smaller with your RV to avoid limitations. It's all personal choice.

TRY TO BE FLEXIBLE

With some experience you will find a travel planning schedule that works for you, but don't feel as though you need to plan every little detail. That can feel like a militant schedule and not at all relaxing. When planning your travels stay mindful of a pace that feels comfortable for you and your companions, including pets. We like to have a general idea of our travels a few months in advance and may have some key reservations in place, but it's not unusual for us to move the dates around slightly, and we've never found ourselves with nowhere to stay.

Be aware that sometimes there will be travel delays or exciting diversions you didn't expect, like a random stop at the OZ Museum in Kansas, which enticed us from a roadside billboard on I-70! You might discover hidden gems when talking to other RVers or locals and add a few stops to your original plan. If you are too rigid in your planning, you may miss out on some very special or memorable stops.

Keep some space and flexibility in your travel schedule for the unexpected. Sometimes going where the path leads you is a more enjoyable experience. In fact, we know some RVers who don't make plans at all and never make advance reservations. They mostly have smaller RVs and a flexible schedule, which makes a big difference. When Marc was working his full-time job, we liked the security of knowing our campsites were booked well in advance so we didn't have to think or worry about where we were going to stay, but now that we are self-employed, have more flexibility in our schedule, and are more experienced RVers, we're more open to traveling without reservations in place—outside of peak times, that is, when it's much easier to find campsites.

TIPS FOR GETTING GOOD DRIVING DIRECTIONS

Driving an RV is different from driving a car. Most RVs are bigger, longer, taller, and heavier, and it generally takes longer to drive or tow an RV than it does to jump in a car and drive. As an RVer, you need to be aware of and plan for a few additional things:

- Driving or towing an RV always takes longer and is more physically and mentally fatiguing than driving a car, as you need to pay extra attention to the road, safety, and other drivers and are generally driving slower. It can be taxing, so don't overdo it, and allow extra time for your arrival. Review and plan your travel route using a road atlas or map. We use and recommend a spiral-bound paper version of the latest *Rand McNally Large Scale Road Atlas*.

- Seek alternate routes to avoid high mountain passes, tunnels, low bridges, and inner-city traffic if possible.

- An RV-specific GPS is a worthwhile investment, especially for larger RVs, so you can program it with your RV's dimensions, and to know which lane to be in for turning. An RV-specific GPS will also provide a more accurate arrival time than your regular car GPS or Google Maps.

Jennifer, 63,
and Kate, 60

**FULL-TIME RVERS FOR 15 MONTHS,
FROM MARCH 2015 TO JUNE 2016**
Website: www.oneyearontheroad.com

"Wherever you
are, you're home."

IT'S ONE THING TO CENTER YOUR LIFE AROUND A JOB THAT fulfills you, but when your job is sucking the life force from you, it's time to consider a whole new paradigm of living.

My wife, Kate, had been working as a social worker in a psych unit for fifteen years, and she was quickly approaching the crispy stage of burnout. My work as a technical writer was less stressful, but the division I worked in was slated to close soon. It was too early for us to retire, but we both knew that if Kate spent much longer at that psych unit, she'd have to check herself in.

We shared a fantasy of hitting the road in an RV and exploring all the nooks and crannies of this vast country. It was a crazy idea, but we figured if we used some of our retirement money now, we could take a year off, see the world, and come back to finish our careers with renewed energy and purpose.

Nine months later we were on the road in a brand-new motorhome, our house packed up and rented out, our golden retriever snuggled between our seats, our Honda CRV rolling behind us, and the world ahead of us. We rejected itineraries and chose instead to see where the wind took us. There were some zigs and zags, but generally we went west to east and back again, and when we returned home fifteen months later, we'd visited forty-seven states and three Canadian provinces. We'd traveled 30,000 miles and visited more than a dozen national parks.

We adopted a newborn kitten in Missouri, went to a Celtic festival in Nova Scotia, dug for diamonds in Arkansas, and dodged tornadoes in Texas. We attended a lesbian festival in Ohio, went to Women's Week in Provincetown, and stayed in a "lesbian village" in the Florida Keys. We made new friends along the way and reconnected with dozens of friends and family all across the country. We came home healthy, happy, and recharged, brimming with stories to tell.

Within a couple of months we both found new jobs we enjoy, but we both look forward to retiring for real in a few more years and revisiting some of the many incredible places we were introduced to during our one year on the road.

- The *Mountain Directories*—East and West—are very useful for route planning and can help you find routes that are safer and place less strain on your RV and its engine and brakes. (These are available as printed paperback books, ebooks and apps. Learn more at www.mountaindirectory.com.)

- *The Next EXIT* is an excellent resource that quickly tells you what's coming up at future exits on interstate highways, like the nearest gas, food, or camping spots. (These are available as printed paperback books or apps. Learn more at www.thenextexit.com.)

- It is helpful to have a good navigator/copilot while driving.

- Try to arrive at your destination well before sunset so you can set up your site in the daylight.

Many RVers use Google Maps, Apple Maps, or a regular car GPS unit for directions when driving their RV. These are okay but not ideal, as the app or GPS will think you are a car and may suggest routes that are inappropriate and unsafe for your RV. An RV-specific GPS is more likely (though not always guaranteed) to choose an appropriate route. Trust us; we learned this the hard way, but no damage was done. That said, no GPS is perfect, so don't blindly follow the instructions. Sometimes road conditions change, and other times the database in the GPS may be out of date. Pay attention to road signs, especially when approaching low bridges or tunnels. More diligent route planners might also use apps like Google Maps satellite view to have a look at gas stations or other destinations en route, to get a feel for how easy they will be to access with their RV. This is especially important if traveling solo. If you have a good navigator traveling with you, some of this research can be done while en route, but it is still wise to have a general idea of what to expect in your travel day before you start rolling, to avoid any nasty surprises.

Follow the Rule of Twos
Many RVers follow the Rule of Twos:

- Don't drive more than 200 miles in a day.
- Drive no longer than two hours at a time.
- Arrive by two p.m. local time.
- Stay at least two nights.

It's not a hard and fast rule, but it's considered a good general guideline for optimal comfort and safety.

WHERE TO STAY

When we first hit the road, we had no idea how many RV parks, campgrounds, and free public lands there were all around the country! We'd never paid attention before, but if you keep an eye open, you'll start seeing RV campgrounds and free camping options everywhere you look. There are a lot more options for parking and camping with your RV than you are probably even aware of. Let's start by getting you acquainted with your options for RV parks and campgrounds.

- **National parks:** There are more than 130 parks you can camp in. These are very popular, so it can be tricky getting reservations, especially during holidays. Be prepared to book well in advance to guarantee a campsite, or arrive early to take a chance on securing a 'first come, first served' site. Good luck!

- **State, city, and municipal parks:** Choose from thousands around the country.

- **Private RV parks and campgrounds:** You'll find these just about everywhere, ranging in size, style, price, and amenities. You can save substantially on your nightly fees by joining a camping discount club or membership-based campground network.

- **RV resorts:** You will find plenty of moderate to upscale RV resorts, too, especially in popular areas. There are huge resorts in desirable snowbird locations where people visit or hunker down in the winter. These resorts offer amazing amenities and close-knit communities because people come back to the same parks year after year and stay for months at a time.

- **Core of Engineers (COE) parks:** Find campsites at one of over 450 COE Parks around the country, which are serviced by the US Army Corps of Engineers.

- **Military bases:** These are available to qualifying current and former military personnel, usually on military bases located around the country.

Have you ever envisioned what your campsite will be like? Do you picture yourself predominantly staying inside national park campgrounds or state and city parks? What about private RV parks or upscale RV resorts? Or would you prefer being in more wooded, rustic campgrounds? Maybe you are retired military and plan to spend time on military bases to make the most of that benefit. All the choices have their pros and cons, but most of them will require a bit of forethought depending on when you are going to stay and the type of RV you travel in. Check out AllStays.com, Campendium.com, CampgroundViews.com, RVParkReviews.com, *Big Rigs Best Bets* (www.big-rigs-rv.com), TripAdvisor.com, do a *Google* search for reviews, and read blogs for RV park and resort reviews and photos. You'll find more than 3,000 video tours (including 360 VR tours) of RV parks and campgrounds at CampgroundViews.com, and reviewers at Campendium.com report on cell coverage for various carriers at many locations.

CAVEATS ABOUT NATIONAL PARKS

We often hear people talk about how they plan to stay in national parks a lot of the time. They might even buy a smaller RV because they hear that some parks have difficulty accommodating RVs over 32 feet (especially in California). Though it is true that larger RVs will have a harder time because there are fewer large sites than small ones, it's not impossible in many parks. Around 70 percent of national parks are reportedly able to accommodate RVs up to 40 feet in length, and that percentage drops to 17 percent for RVs over 40 feet. Regardless of length, it is often tricky securing reservations in national parks unless you book way in advance, as they are so popular, and they can be a challenge for pet owners since dogs are not allowed on most trails. So you might end up staying inside national parks less often than you expect. Choose your RV size based on what you will feel comfortable living in and where you plan on staying the majority of the time. Don't let 10 percent of your destinations affect your living space the other 90 percent of the time. That said, if you find an RV that meets all your needs and those of your travel companions and it is less than 32 feet long, you will generally have an easier time finding places to park it.

Don't worry; if you have your heart set on a bigger RV, you can still visit most, if not all, of the places on your list, but you may need to stay outside of the national park. There are privately owned RV parks in the areas near many major attractions that are more likely to accommodate larger RVs and will also be more likely to have full hookup sites and reliable cell coverage.

FREE CAMPING AND OVERNIGHT PARKING

There are actually many options for free camping. Some are situated out in nature, while others are located in more convenient and populated areas, and these can be handy to stop for a night along your route to get some rest after a big driving day. Let's go through the options.

FREE CAMPING ON PUBLIC LANDS: BOONDOCKING AND DRY CAMPING

If you like the idea of being able to boondock (or as it's commonly known, camp out in the "boonies"), you'll use your RV's onboard resources to camp off the grid in peaceful, scenic locations in nature, without being hooked up at an RV park or campground. You will find free, undeveloped public lands and wide open spaces, mainly in the western parts of the US. The Bureau of Land Management (BLM) manages much of the land that RVers park on, and usually allows you to stay up to fourteen days in a location at a time. We spoke a bit about RV systems in Chapter 3, and the ability of most RVs to comfortably camp off-grid for at least a few days, and some that can do it for a couple of weeks or much longer. You will need to conserve power and water usage, but with a few lifestyle adaptations or some modifications to your RV (like installing solar and better batteries), you may enjoy spending the majority of your time unplugged.

WHERE TO FIND FREE OVERNIGHT PARKING

Sometimes you might be in the middle of a big travel day and simply need a place to get off the road and sleep. Or you may seek out some unique destinations, just for the experience. There are a number of places you can park your RV for free overnight, almost always without hookups, so let's introduce you to your options.

Here are some resources for finding great free camping spots:

- AllStays.com
- BLM.gov
- Campendium.com
- FreeCampsites.net
- Frugal-RV-Travel.com

You can also download apps for *AllStays*, *Campendium*, and US Public Lands by Two Steps Beyond to keep these great resources at your fingertips.

In addition to those resources, consider these options:

- **Rest areas:** These are usually located off major interstates and highways, and are a great option for taking a rest or having a bite to eat, and some—but not all—allow free overnight parking.

- **Walmart, truck stops, casinos, and more:** Many large chains, such as Walmart, Cracker Barrel, Cabela's, and Kmart—as well as casinos, truck stops, and even some shopping malls—allow RVers to park overnight in their large parking lots. Be aware that rules vary among locations, and some city and county ordinances may override the business's policies. Be sure to talk to somebody like a manager, employee, or security guard to get permission before just assuming it is okay, or you might get a knock on your door in the middle of the night and need to move along, which can be unsettling and ruin the whole point of stopping in the first place. If you choose to overnight in a parking lot generously offered by one of these companies, be respectful. Don't put your leveling jacks down, don't put your slides out, don't run your generator, and don't put your chairs or BBQ out either. It is designed to be a safe place to park your RV overnight, not a campsite. Go inside to support the business with a purchase, and try to leave the area cleaner than it was when you arrived, so that businesses continue to offer this valuable service to RVers in the future. This style of overnighting isn't for everyone. You may be parked near a loud refrigeration truck or hear traffic throughout the night. But these lots are generally safe, convenient, and welcome places to stop and break up a long drive, without having to pay for a campground. If you do want to put out your slides, get comfortable, and plug in your appliances, especially if it's hot or cold and you don't have sufficient energy storage in your batteries for comfortable overnight stays, you may prefer to stay in an RV park. But it's handy to know that these free overnight places may be available if you need them.

- **Wineries, farms, attractions, and golf clubs:** Does the thought of waking up among vineyards, on a farm, or by a museum, golf course, or other attraction appeal to you? You can join organizations like Harvest Hosts and RV Golf Club—which offer free overnight parking for fully self-contained RVs at hundreds of unique locations around the country—for a small annual membership fee that pays for itself in your first one or two stays.

- **Private property:** RVers are a friendly bunch, and there are many who welcome other RVers to park overnight on their private property. Meet fellow travelers, share stories, sleep well, and make new friends through Boondockers Welcome, a site that connects hosts with RVers looking for a place to spend the night.

SAVE MONEY WITH RV AND CAMPING MEMBERSHIPS

One of the best ways to stretch your dollars as an RVer is to join one or more RV organizations and camping memberships. You'll enjoy benefits and discounts that can literally save you hundreds, if not thousands, of dollars. We'll go into a few that we feel are worth checking out so you can decide which one may be a good fit for your needs.

RV CLUBS WITH MEMBER BENEFITS AND DISCOUNTS

These are the major RV clubs known for offering member benefits, including discounts on RV parking and travel.

- **Escapees and Xscapers RV Clubs:** We mentioned the community benefits of being a member of Escapees and their sub-club Xscapers in Chapter 5. They are a total support network for all RVers, with benefits including 15–50 percent discounts on commercial RV parks; access to deeded lots, lease lots, and member-owned co-op parks; mail-forwarding and domicile services; an RV weight safety program; a magazine; an online job center; discounts to products and services; education; a national rally; and local events. Escapees also provides advocacy for the rights of RVers and runs the CARE program (providing continued assistance for retired RVers), and Xscapers provides a strong, supportive community for working-age, active, and adventurous RVers. Membership is $39.95 per year for US residents and $49.95 for Canada/Mexico residents.

- **FMCA:** Also mentioned for its community benefits in Chapter 5, FMCA is a long-standing club for RV owners with a focus on rights and advocacy, plus many member benefits, including a mail-forwarding service, an emergency medical evacuation program, active forums, international conventions and local rallies, education, a magazine, anti-theft decals, international travel insurance, discounts on cell phone plans, fuel, RV technical and roadside assistance, and a tire savings program. Membership is open to owners of motorhomes and towable RVs and is $50 per year.

- **Good Sam Club:** Owned by Camping World, Good Sam offers member discounts on RV parks and campgrounds, RV shows, and RV products and services at Camping World, and fuel discounts at Pilot/Flying J. They also offer roadside assistance, finance, insurance, and a free online trip planner. Membership is $27 per year (less with bonus certificates and/or multiyear memberships).

- **AIM Club:** The All Inclusive Motorhome Club is a relatively new club for owners of any Class A, B, or C motorhome. They offer member discounts on emergency roadside service, emergency ambulance service, vehicle insurance, and auto purchases. They provide information and education through the AIM website, *Facebook* page, newsletters, forums, and training at AIM rallies. Membership is $35 a year.

- **Explorers RV Club of Canada:** This is the largest Canadian RV camping club, serving all RVers with member benefits including discounts on camping fees, insurance, hotels, road travel, and emergency roadside service; free subscription to *Canadian RVing* magazine; and a national rally. Membership for one year (in Canadian dollars) is $47 for Canada, $60 for the US, and $100 for international members.

RV CAMPING MEMBERSHIPS AND DISCOUNT CLUBS

- **Thousand Trails:** This membership-based camping network has more than eighty campgrounds in twenty-two states plus British Columbia, Canada, and is popular with full-time RVers. Various levels of memberships allow members to camp for free for up to twenty-eight days in each park in five regions called "zones." The Optional Trails Collection program allows up to fourteen-night stays at 110 additional RV resorts. We use Thousand Trails a lot—get our tips, reviews, and recommendations at RVLove.com. Membership starts at $575 for one year (less during promotions).

- **Passport America:** This discount camping club offers 50 percent off regular rates at more than 1,800 campgrounds in the US, Canada, and Mexico; a free online directory (printed directory available for a fee); rallies; and RV caravan trips. Some properties have limitations during holidays and/or weekends. Membership costs $44 for one year.

- **KOA:** Kampgrounds of America has almost 500 locations across the US and Canada. You can buy a loyalty card to save 10 percent on daily rates and earn camping points for discounts on future stays. Membership costs $30 for one year.

- **Harvest Hosts:** Members with self-contained RVs can explore Harvest Hosts' network of more than 500 host wineries, farms, breweries, distilleries, museums, and attractions, to visit and stay overnight for free. Membership is $49 for one year (save $4 with code RVLOVE17).

- **Boondockers Welcome:** Park overnight on private property. Meet fellow travelers, share stories, sleep well, and make new friends with this site that connects hosts with RVers looking for a place to spend the night for free. You can be hosted and/or host other RVers on your own property; the website simply connects you. Membership is $30 for one year ($15 for hosts).

CROSSING THE BORDER: RVING TO CANADA AND MEXICO

There are forty-eight amazing contiguous states to visit in the United States, and we hope you get to see them all! But you don't need to stop there—you can also cross the US border with your RV to visit Canada and Mexico. There's a bit more planning required than simply traveling between US states, but it's absolutely doable. If you're a US citizen or resident, you won't need a visa to enter Canada, but you will need a valid passport. Even if you just want to drive over the International Rainbow Bridge to see Niagara Falls from the Canadian side, it'll be worth it! Of course, if you decide to RV to Alaska, you'll need to drive through Canada to get there. Take your time; Canada is beautiful!

> "Travel is more than the seeing of sights; it is a change that goes on, deep and permanent, in the ideas of living."
>
> —*Miriam Beard, UK author*

You will need valid vehicle registration, valid insurance, and your US driver's license. All of Canada's ten provinces speak English, except Quebec, where they speak both French and English—but beware, their signs are in French! Speed signs are shown in kilometers instead of miles (1.6 kilometers equal 1 mile), so keep an eye on your speed! Many people dream of driving the Trans-Canada Highway by RV, which stretches more than 4,800 miles from the Pacific to the Atlantic Ocean, exploring all ten provinces along the way from beautiful British Columbia to nautical Nova Scotia. Discover Canada-specific trip planning, tips, and campground reservations at the https://gorving.ca/trip-planning and https://us-keepexploring.canada.travel, and make campground reservations at Parks Canada.

Before you drive up to any of the Canadian border crossings, you'll need to ensure that you are carrying the correct documentation for all passengers—including minors and pets—and that you are not carrying anything on

board your RV that is not allowed. Always check the customs and border crossing websites of the country you're departing from and heading to for the most up-to-date information, but in general you should anticipate having to leave some things behind. Check on the rules and limitations surrounding fruits, vegetables, meats, and spices. You'll be restricted on how much alcohol and tobacco you can bring in, and you definitely can't take firewood or illegal drugs, including marijuana.

Canada also has strict rules around firearms, and crossing into Canada without the proper permits for guns can land you in jail, so don't take this lightly (see www.cbp.gov/travel/us-citizens/canada-mexico-travel). If you carry firearms in your RV, start doing your homework a good three months in advance of your travels, to understand what's allowed, what isn't, and the correct permits and documentation, so you can create an action plan. For example, hunting rifles may be allowed into the country with proper permits, but not handguns. Check the rules, get the proper permits and documentation, and be prepared. Canadians are generally friendly, but yes, sometimes they may bring agents with dogs onboard to thoroughly search your RV, while making you wait outside. Stay calm and follow the rules for their country.

Mexico also has strict rules (see www.cbp.gov/travel/us-citizens/canada-mexico-travel), and the first line on the US Customs and Border Protection website regarding travel to Mexico is "Warning: It's Illegal to Carry Firearms or Ammo Into Mexico." Do not plan on taking firearms into Mexico at all.

You don't usually need special insurance to drive into Canada, but you will definitely need to purchase special "Mexico auto liability insurance" south of the US border to protect yourself in the event of an accident, to cover damages that you may cause with your vehicle or to other people's property, and/or bodily injuries to other people. You are liable for the cost of all damages caused, whether it's through insurance or out of pocket, so the bottom line is not to drive your vehicle in Mexico without proper Mexican liability coverage, as it may not only be potentially financially devastating, but it could also land you in legal trouble. Coverage of at least USD $300,000 is recommended. While we have traveled to Canada with our RV, we have not yet traveled to Mexico and therefore cannot speak to it from personal experience. However, we know many RVers who have safely traveled to Mexico and back with their RV—some do it regularly—and Mexico remains one of the top winter destinations in the world. It is generally recommended that you travel into Mexico as part of a group with other RVers—or even as part of an organized caravan adventure group—but we have heard of a few who are comfortable going solo. Baja, California is a popular destination for RVers wanting to winter in Mexico (see www.discoverbaja.com/go/driving-mexico for more information).

OTHER TRAVEL OPTIONS: CHEAP FLIGHTS, CRUISES, TRAVELING ON POINTS, AND VOLUNTEERISM

Have RV, will travel…anywhere! Don't think for a moment that all of your adventures will be limited to road trips from now on—your RV provides a fantastic, mobile, and cost-effective base for other kinds of travel and exploring too. No matter how much we love our RV lifestyle, we have found it's still nice to get away for a break every now and then, to have a different kind of experience. It doesn't have to cost much either. With a bit of creativity and flexibility, you could travel even more for less, as living in an RV can actually make it easier and less expensive to enjoy some of the other types of travel you may have done in the past. Let's take a look at some of the advantages.

TRAVELING FROM AN RV IS LESS WORK

When you have a traditional home, you often need to arrange for someone to housesit, bring in your mail, take care of the gardens and yard, or otherwise keep up the property and make it appear lived in. When you live in an RV, you can either put it in storage or, in some cases, lock it up and leave it safely set up in your campsite at an RV park while you travel elsewhere. If you have pets, you may need to board them or arrange for a pet sitter, but that's no different than it would be at home.

WHY WE LOVE RVING

Erik, 38, and Kala, 31

FULL-TIME RVERS SINCE APRIL 2015

Website: www.livinlite.net
YouTube: www.livinlite.net
Instagram: @livinlite_net
Facebook: LivinLite.net

"Since hitting the road, our mobile lifestyle has allowed us to focus more on our relationship, our family, and the things that matter most to us, while giving us the financial flexibility to cut a decade off our retirement date."

IN THE SUMMER OF 2014 WE HAD "MADE IT" FOR ALL INTENTS and purposes. We owned multiple properties and businesses, drove fancy cars, and lived in a five-bedroom house in a highly affluent part of Connecticut. Erik owned a successful IT services company, and Kala was a successful operations administrator for a global bank. But...we couldn't have been more miserable despite living the "American Dream."

We both worked sixty-hour weeks and spent hours each day commuting or stuck in traffic, and the cost of living in Southern Connecticut meant that, despite all our success, we were still somehow living paycheck to paycheck. We were slaves to our possessions, being strangled by monthly payments for houses, utilities, cars, student loans, and increasing credit card debt. Most people around us seemed to be in the same boat, and everyone kept talking about how they would live their life in some far-off future when they had earned enough, saved enough, done enough. This concept was slowly eating us alive, and worst of all, we found we were working so hard that we weren't spending time on the things that mattered most to us—our family, our relationship, and our own health.

Thus began the search for a solution. It wasn't as simple as just deciding to live a different life. We had spent so much of our lives "reacting" to the world around us that we had no idea what we really wanted out of life. It started to become clear that in order to find so-called happiness, we needed to create an environment where we could first find ourselves.

The idea of packing up and hitting the road took hold of us and couldn't be stopped until we made it a reality. We spent nearly six months researching and planning our departure, deciding to keep our home and find tenants to cover our mortgage and keep an eye on it while we traveled. We sold everything else—the cars, motorcycles, furniture, and electronics—and kept only the items we could tow or fit in our RV, plus some keepsakes we deemed important enough to keep in a small storage unit.

More than three years later, we couldn't be happier. We still work full-time, but the time spent working is more focused and much more productive. As a result, our work performance is the highest it's ever been, and the financial freedom that our mobile lifestyle has afforded us now allows us to save more than half our annual income. When work is done, we leave it behind, going outside to find ourselves just about anywhere—the weather is great, and our neighbors are on permanent vacation. We spend more time on ourselves and our relationship, got engaged in 2016, and married in the fall of 2018—and we have no plans to return to a traditional lifestyle.

YOU CAN DRIVE TO CHEAPER FLIGHTS

The second advantage to travel while RVing is that you can shop around for the best airfares and choose to fly out of whichever airport has the best rates, as opposed to always needing to fly out of the airport nearest to your home. When you live in an RV, you just move your home to the airport offering the best price, schedule, or campground to fit in with your travel needs. For example: when convenient, we like flying in and out of Phoenix, Arizona, as it's a major airport with lots of flight and carrier options, there are plenty of campgrounds nearby where we can safely leave our RV, and above all, we often find really cheap airfares to and from Phoenix! We've also flown out of Las Vegas, Palm Springs, and Dallas. Shopping around for cheap airfares in cities that make sense for us on our travels has literally paid off.

TAKE ADVANTAGE OF LAST-MINUTE DISCOUNTED CRUISES

If you like going on cruises, living in an RV and having control over your schedule can add up to huge discounts. As many people who live in port cities know, cruise ships often heavily discount their fares for their cruises during the last days before sailing. This is because cruise ships make a lot of money from passengers through drink sales, shopping, tours, and onboard casinos. Most of a cruise ship's expenses—like staff, fuel, and docking fees—will remain virtually the same for a cruise, regardless of how many passengers they have onboard, so they are most profitable when the ship is full. If you like cruising or have a particular cruise destination in mind, consider staying in your RV near major port cities that align with your travel goals, and keep an eye out for last-minute cruise deals. You can sign up for cruise line email announcements to nab them as soon as they come out. In September 2017 our RV was parked in a campground in British Columbia, Canada, about an hour and a half drive east of Vancouver, a major port city. We had always wanted to visit Alaska, being our fiftieth US state visited, and when looking for options for us to have a little anniversary getaway, Julie came across a seven-day one-way cruise from Vancouver, BC, to Seward, Alaska, for $399 per person. That included all of our meals, cabin, and entertainment; we just had to cover the tax and port charges (a couple hundred dollars each), personal spending, and one-way airfares from Anchorage back to Vancouver. And because we had accumulated credit card points from our RV travels and life, we were able to stay for three nights at a nice hotel in Anchorage for free, as the airfares were much cheaper three days after the rest of the cruise passengers had left. We were able to work remotely from the hotel room—and even the cruise ship some—and integrate that into our mobile life. We had a blast, and it was a very special and affordable way to not only celebrate our wedding anniversary but also complete our fiftieth state visited.

USE POINTS AND DISCOUNTS TO TRAVEL ALMOST FOR FREE

We did a similar thing the year before when we flew to Hawaii on cheap flights, stayed on Maui mostly for free using hotel and credit card points, and rented a Mustang convertible for exploring—again, using our points, making our ten days in Hawaii a very affordable getaway indeed! We have credit cards that earn us extra points for travel-related spending—like campgrounds, RV parks, restaurants, and fuel—so our everyday RV lifestyle helps us accumulate points very quickly, even faster than we can use them sometimes!

RV TERMS TO KNOW

travel hacking: Earning and using credit card and travel points to travel, virtually for free.

We have been inspired by and learned a great deal from our full-time RVing friends Robert and Veronica (you read their story in Chapter 8), former air traffic controllers who have mastered the art of travel hacking. They frequently use credit card and travel points to travel extensively around the world for next to nothing—while using their RV as their US home base. They regularly fly internationally (sometimes first class) and stay in very nice hotels—usually for free, using their credit card points and air miles—they just pay the taxes. They simply pay to either put their RV into storage or leave it hooked up in a campground while they travel and visit family all around the world, instead of worrying about the responsibilities, concern, or expense of maintaining a property while they're gone. They don't miss their old house or the high property taxes they used to pay, and have found an incredibly resourceful way to maximize their activities and spending to support a lifestyle that they love. By combining RVing around the US with international travel, they are now better off financially than they were before and have a blast doing it.

VOLUNTEERISM

We touched on RV volunteering in Chapter 5 when discussing community. Let's recap on that briefly here as it relates to ease of travel. When natural disasters or other events leave people adversely affected, those with the desire and ability to lend a hand can relocate to the area in need and provide assistance without requiring housing because they bring their homes with them. There are also international volunteer and relief efforts that you can participate in—and leave your RV in storage or at a campground—for causes like the Red Cross and Habitat for Humanity, or maybe you like the idea of building schools, hospitals, or housing (like Earthships) in third-world countries. The possibilities are endless.

Our friend Clint is a solo RVer who was forced into medical retirement at age thirty-five. Luckily his condition left him still physically capable of travel, and he spends a lot of time volunteering for the American Red Cross deploying to various disasters across the United States. He has also taken temporary paid positions when it has fit his travels and plans to deploy to disasters in his RV when he can.

OFF AND DRIVING

So, are you inspired to get back to your travel planning now…and perhaps even expand your itinerary beyond what you initially imagined?

As you can see, with an RV, just about anything is possible. And while trip planning takes time, it's a rewarding challenge, and a fun part of the adventure that the RV lifestyle offers. It's about so much more than the places you'll visit and the things you'll do; it's also about where you'll go within yourself. After all of our travels and the amazing places we've seen, perhaps the most impactful thing of all has been how RVing has changed us, for the better.

CONCLUSION

**"Every day is a journey,
and the journey itself is home."**
—*Matsuo Bashō, Japanese poet*

Congratulations! We truly hope you have enjoyed this phase of your journey as much as we have! By now you should feel as though you have a solid understanding of the RV life and a plan to get you on your way. We know there's been a lot of information to take in, and your learning journey is far from over, but you can feel confident knowing that you're off to an excellent start with your new RV lifestyle with this road map to help you get there.

Refer back to this book often to recap on the information in each chapter as you reach each mile marker along the way. This isn't something you need to rush; it isn't a race. You will find the right RV to suit your lifestyle and a timeline that works for you. But don't wait too long; there's a whole world out there, and the open road is calling!

You'll be happy to know that your resources don't end with the final chapter of this book. Although we've packed a lot of great information into this book, we've only scratched the surface of all there is to know about RV life. So we've created some free bonus content for you to help you continue your learning! Head on over to https://rvlove.com/book-bonus-content and sign up for even more useful information and resources, including more RVer profiles, extra links, free downloads, expert interviews, gear recommendations, plus special offers and exclusive discounts.

And if you're ready for an even deeper dive, we invite you to join us and many fellow RVers and RV experts at RV Success School, where you will discover our online courses "Hit the Road the Right Way," "Choosing the Right RV for You," and more. There are videos, lessons, workbooks, and webinars to continue your education and guide you to making great decisions.

Connect with us and our awesome community of RVLovers at our blog, RVLove.com, on YouTube, and on social media—Facebook, Instagram, Twitter, Pinterest, and RVillage—and jump onto our RVLove email list for updates, info, and offers that you won't get anywhere else. You can also find us at EpicNomadTV.com, where you can watch the RV Nomads movie for free.

Of course, you are always welcome to join us and hang out with thousands of other RV nomads within the ENTV app and in person at RVNomadFEST live events. And you never know—we may just serendipitously cross paths at a campground, at an RV rally, or out in the middle of nowhere at a scenic boondocking location sometime.

Your eyes have been opened to a whole other world of possibilities and a new way to live that's ultimately all about freedom. Once you hit the road, you may find that there's no going back, for RVing changes you. You may hang up the keys someday, but you will never be the same again. You'll be able to look back and say, "I lived my dream, I had the adventure of a lifetime, and I'd do it all over again." Wishing you happy trails and every success! We'll see you online and on the road.

Best of Life,
Marc and Julie

DISCOVER MORE AT OUR WEBSITE

RVLOVe.com

GET FREE BOOK BONUSES — RVLove.com/book-bonus-content

SIGN UP FOR EMAIL UPDATES — RVLove.com/sign-up-for-more

CONTINUE LEARNING — RVSuccessSchool.com

WATCH THE MOVIE — watch.epicnomadtv.com

CONNECT WITH US ON SOCIAL MEDIA

www.youtube.com/rvlove

www.facebook.com/rvlovetv

www.instagram.com/rvlovetravel

www.pinterest.com/rvlovetravel

www.twitter.com/rvlovetravel

www.rvlove.com/myENTV

www.rvlove.com/rvillage

INDEX

Action plans, 11, 31–58, 243. See also Trip planning
Airports, 246–47
Apps
  banking app, 217
  Countdown app, 50
  ENTV app, 130, 251
  health apps, 162
  location apps, 167, 228, 231
  medical apps, 152
  pet sitter apps, 107, 182
  social network apps, 130–31, 251
  travel apps, 167, 185–86, 223, 228, 231, 236
  weather apps, 88

Banking, 208, 216–17
Baril, Dennis, 172
Bashō, Matsuo, 250
Beard, Miriam, 241
Bennett, Ellen, 197
Bennett, Julie, 9–10, 19, 50, 55, 127, 154, 164, 177, 246
Bennett, Marc, 9–10, 59, 71, 98, 113, 122, 152, 164, 167, 173, 175, 177, 228
Biking, 75, 161–63, 165, 224–25
Boondocking, 20–21, 33–35, 135, 224–26, 236–40. See also Off-grid living
Border crossings, 155–56, 241–44
Braga, Jennifer, 111, 165
Braga, Jerome, 127, 165
Breakdowns/repairs, 25–26, 90–92
Brown, Dan, 117
Brown, Lisa, 117
Budget, creating, 32–39, 42–43
Bus conversions, 60, 113, 135, 185

Cahill, Tim, 119
Campbell, Joseph, 95
Campervan, 70
Campground hosts, 180, 185, 237, 241
Campgrounds, 105, 136, 227, 232–33, 236–37. See also RV parks
Caravan, 70, 240, 244
Career, changing, 96–97, 177–78. See also Work
Cell phones, 110, 167

Cellular connections, 186–90
Children
  border crossings with, 241–43
  educating, 21, 28, 48, 53, 99, 105, 165, 206
  experiences for, 99, 103–5
  personalities of, 103
  traveling with, 93, 99–105, 125, 165
Class A motorhome, 60–61, 68
Class B motorhome, 60–61, 68
Class C motorhome, 62–63, 68
Class Super C motorhome, 62–63
Clubs, 131–37, 185, 200, 232, 238–41
Clutter, 53–56, 110–11
Communication, 102–3, 108–10, 139–40
Communities, 28, 130–42, 147, 208, 232. See also Clubs
Consumerism, 50, 53
Cooking tips, 159–61
Corps of Engineers (COE) parks, 232. See also Campgrounds
Credit cards, 42, 216–19
Cruises, 246–47

Debt, paying off, 42–43
Dental care, 155–56
Diet/nutrition, 159–61
Domicile, establishing, 105, 147, 197–213, 219, 238
Downsizing, 18–19, 31, 50–58, 96–97
Downtime, 105, 108–9, 194–95
Dry camping, 20–21, 33–35, 135, 224–26, 236–40. See also Off-grid living
Dunphy, Chris, 185, 189, 190

Emergency care, 149–50. See also Medical considerations
Emotional considerations, 93–116, 119–64
Emotional journey, 10, 50–52
Epic Nomad TV (ENTV), 10, 130, 184, 251
Ethical considerations, 207
Events, 131, 134–37, 225–26, 238–40, 251
Exercise, 161–67
Expectations, 28, 184–86

Faith-based groups, 142, 147

Family
  communities for, 28, 131–34, 137
  leaving, 96–98, 119–20
  staying in touch with, 119–25
  traveling with, 93, 99–111, 125, 165
Fifth wheel RV, 64–65, 68, 73, 88. See also RVs
Financial considerations, 19–21, 24–28, 32–43, 60–80. See also Banking
Firearms, 167, 243
First aid kits, 155
Fitness, 161–67
Free camping, 233, 236–37, 240. See also Dry camping
Friends
  conversing with, 139–40
  leaving, 96–98, 119–20
  making new, 119–42
  staying in touch with, 119–25
Frugal RVers, 37, 135, 137, 157, 233, 236–37
Fuel costs, 25, 35–36

Glamping, 47–48
Goals, defining, 18–22, 30, 36–40, 42–53
Gondeck, Dawn, 43, 141
Gondeck, Mike, 141
Goodman, Ellen, 18
GPS locations, 167, 186, 223, 228, 231
Groups, 28, 130–42, 147, 208, 232. See also Clubs
Guillebeau, Chris, 207
Gym workouts, 161–62

Habits, healthy, 156–64
Healthcare professionals, 147–50, 152–54
Health considerations, 143–67
Health insurance, 144–48, 165, 200, 204
Health issues, 148–50, 152–56, 165
Health share programs, 145, 147
Healthy eating, 159–61
Healthy routines, 156–64
Healthy tips, 143–67
Hiking, 11, 102, 135–36, 161–62, 165–67, 224–25
Hill, Kate, 229
Hobbies, 100–102, 113, 129–31, 136
Holistic healthcare, 154–55

Home medical kits, 154–55
Home remedies, 152–55
Homeschooling, 21, 28, 48, 53, 99, 105, 165
House, renting, 39, 40, 97
House, selling, 31, 38–40, 96–97

Illnesses, 148–50. See also Health considerations
Income taxes, 201, 205, 219
Insurance, health, 144–48, 165, 200, 204
Insurance, vehicle, 36, 80, 204, 243–44
Internet connections, 186–90

Job, leaving, 21, 96–97, 177–78. See also Work
Jury duty, 200, 210

Krishnamurti, Jiddu, 143

Lakein, Alan, 31
Launch date, planning, 49–50, 58
Legal considerations, 167, 197–219, 243–44
LGBTQ RVers, 137
Licenses, 60, 198, 204–8, 214, 241
Living expenses, 35–38, 43
Living space, 25, 60–67, 70–72, 100–117

Mail-forwarding service, 197, 205–16, 238
Maps, 167, 186, 228, 231
McCauley, Erik, 190, 245
McCauley, Kala, 190, 245
Meal planning, 160–61
Medical conditions, 148–56, 165
Medical considerations, 143–67
Medical consultations, 147–50, 152–54
Medical insurance, 144–48, 165, 200, 204
Medical kits, 154–55
Medical records, 148
Medical tourism, 155–56
Medicare, 144, 145
Medications, 148–49
Membership clubs, 131–37, 185, 200, 232, 238–41
Meyer, Jennifer, 229
Military bases, 232
Miller, Henry, 250
Morton, Caitlin, 23, 110
Morton, Tom, 23
Moss, Marissa, 125
Moss, Nathan, 125

Motorcycling, 75, 117, 131, 136
Motorhomes, 60–72, 88–89. See also RVs
Myths, 24–28

National parks, 102, 105–6, 161, 221–27, 232–33
Natural remedies, 152–55
Nutrition, 159–61

Off-grid living, 20–24, 33–35, 107, 113–17, 157, 236. See also Boondocking
Olesh, Becky, 83
Olesh, Tom, 83
Organization tips, 50–58, 110–11
Overnight parking, 233, 236–37, 240

Paperwork, digitizing, 57–58
Patience, 102–3, 130, 184–86
Pets
  boarding, 107, 244
  border crossings with, 241–43
  events for, 136
  safety of, 106–7
  sitter for, 107, 182
  traveling with, 23, 51, 106–7, 117, 136, 227, 244
  vaccination of, 106
  vet records for, 106–7
Photos, digitizing, 57–58
Physical activity, 161–67
Positives, focus on, 100–103, 156, 164–65, 172
Possessions, downsizing, 18–19, 50, 52–57, 96–97
Practical considerations, 169–95, 197–219, 221–28
Prescriptions, 148–49. See also Medical considerations
Priorities, setting, 44–48
Property taxes, 28, 38–39, 43, 201, 204, 247

Radio communication, 110
Rallies, 131, 134–35, 137, 238, 240
Registration, 36, 80, 206, 207
Relocating, 21, 96–98, 177–78, 248
Repairs, 25–26, 36, 90–92
Reservations, making, 226–28, 232–33, 241
Residence, primary, 198. See also Domicile, establishing
Riley, Stephen, 99
Riley, Tanya, 99
Roadschooling, 21, 28, 48, 53, 99, 105, 165
Roadside assistance, 90–92, 238
Roberts, Steven, 185

Roosevelt, Eleanor, 222
Rule of Twos, 231
RVgeeks, 191
RV lifestyle. See also RV parks; RVs
  benefits of, 16–24
  choosing, 16–22, 30, 44–48
  cost of, 35–38, 43
  decisions about, 31–58
  designing, 44–48
  destinations for, 221–48
  emotional considerations, 93–116, 119–64
  expectations of, 28, 184–86
  financial considerations, 19–21, 24–28, 32–43, 60–80
  fitness considerations, 161–67
  full-time RVing, 15–30, 35–43, 51, 68–72, 83, 91–99, 103–31, 137–43, 157, 165, 178–91, 194–222, 229, 245–47
  getting started, 13, 31–58
  health considerations, 143–67
  legal considerations, 167, 197–219, 243–44
  living expenses, 35–38, 43
  logistics of, 108–10
  medical considerations, 143–67
  membership clubs, 131–37, 185, 200, 232, 238–41
  myths about, 24–28
  nutrition considerations, 159–61
  organization tips for, 50–58, 110–11
  part-time RVing, 13, 16, 20, 40, 83, 131, 178, 185, 197
  planning, 11, 31–58, 221–48
  popularity of, 19–21
  practical considerations, 169–95, 197–219, 221–28
  quiz on, 30
  safety tips for, 84–92, 106–7, 164–67, 228–31
  seasonal considerations, 88, 107, 180–81, 226–27
  small-space living, 25, 60–67, 70–72, 100–117
  success with, 31–58, 100–117
  supplies for, 52–53
  timeframe for, 48–50
  transitioning to, 43, 95–116, 162–64, 169–85, 201, 245
RVLove, 9–10, 113, 130, 177, 182, 240, 250–51
RV Nomads, 10, 130, 135, 182, 251
RV parks
  amenities in, 33, 37, 47, 232, 240
  discounts for, 232, 238–40
  fees for, 33, 35, 232, 238–40
  finding, 232–33, 236–37

hookups in, 22, 47, 82–87, 186, 226, 233
pets and, 106, 136, 227
RV resorts, 33, 37, 232, 240
RVs. See also RV lifestyle
breakdowns with, 25–26, 90–92
bunkhouse in, 103, 113, 114
buying, 68–80
choosing, 26, 59–73
cost of, 24, 26, 28, 32, 60–67, 73–80
decorating, 111–17
depreciation of, 28, 32, 73, 75, 77–79, 116
electrical systems in, 82
expense overview of, 37–38
extended service contract on, 75, 79–80
financing, 24, 32, 40, 73, 77–79
finding, 59, 68–73, 76
fuel for, 25, 35–36
inspection of, 75, 79, 206
insurance for, 36, 80, 204, 243–44
layout of, 61–67, 70–72
living expenses, 35–38, 43
living space in, 25, 60–67, 70–72, 100–117
maintenance of, 36, 90–92
mileage of, 25, 36
MSRP of, 68, 73, 78–79
myths about, 24–28
personal touches for, 111–17
propane system in, 84
quality of, 72
registration of, 36, 80, 206, 207
reliability of, 72
renting, 77
repairs on, 25–26, 36, 90–92
safety of, 84–92
size of, 60–68, 88–89
slide-outs in, 60–68, 113
supplies for, 52–53
testing, 71–72
types of, 60–73, 88–89
understanding, 80–89
upgrading, 22, 33–39, 111–17
warranty on, 75, 79
water system in, 82–83
RV Success School, 10, 182, 250

Sabbatical, 40, 150
Safety tips, 84–92, 106–7, 164–67, 228–31

Sales tax, 80, 201
Seasonal considerations, 88, 107, 180–81, 226–27
Second home, 37–38, 78
Self-defense, 167
Self-employed RVers, 144–45, 165, 176–86, 191
Self-sufficiency, 21, 30, 82, 150–55
Shortell, Joanne, 157
Slide-on, 70
Slide-outs, 60–68, 113
Small-space living, 25, 60–67, 70–72, 100–117
Social media, 107–8, 113, 121–22, 130–39, 184–86, 251
Solar power, 33–35, 83, 91, 113, 114, 157, 185–86, 236
Solo RVers, 51, 127, 137, 176, 178, 248
Sontag, Susan, 221
State of domicile, 105, 147, 197–213, 219
State parks, 105, 161, 224–27, 232
Stress, reducing, 9, 18–19, 50, 156–59
Supplies, 52–53
Support network, 93, 97–98, 105, 120, 128–42, 184, 238
Sweeney, Anne, 171

Taxes, income, 201, 205, 219
Taxes, property, 28, 38–39, 43, 201, 204, 247
Taxes, sales, 80, 201
Teamwork, 109–10
Time for self, 105, 108–9
Timeframe, determining, 48–50
Tow vehicle, 24, 36, 64, 68, 73–75, 77, 82, 233
Toy hauler, 66–67, 114
Transitions, 43, 95–116, 162–64, 169–85, 201, 245
Travel destinations. See also Trip planning
airports, 246–47
border crossings, 155–56, 241–44
campgrounds, 232–33, 236–37
cruises, 246–47
driving directions for, 228, 231
experiences for, 224–25
flexibility with, 227–28
guides for, 223, 231, 236
inspiration for, 222–23
must-see destinations, 224
parks, 102, 105–6, 161, 221–27, 232–33
reservations for, 226–28, 232–33, 241
Travel hacking, 247
Travel points, 217, 246–47
Travel trailer, 64–65, 68
Trip planning

action plans, 11, 31–58, 243
choosing routes, 223
driving directions for, 228, 231
experiences for, 224–25
flexibility with, 227–28
launch date, 49–50, 58
making reservations, 226–28, 232–33, 241
must-see destinations, 224
seasonal considerations, 88, 107, 180–81, 226–27
travel apps, 167, 185–86, 223, 228, 231, 236
Truck camper, 66–68, 70
Twain, Mark, 100

Unknowns, 23, 93, 98–100, 117
Urgent care, 149–50

Vaughan, Robert, 205, 247
Vaughan, Veronica, 205, 247
Ve Ard, Cherie, 185, 189, 190
Video calls, 121, 186
Volunteerism, 140, 142, 172, 185, 248. See also Work
Voting eligibility, 200, 205, 208, 210

Weather considerations, 88, 107, 180–81, 226–27
Wells, Bob, 137, 157
White, Allison, 91
White, Daryl (Dee), 213
White, Michael, 213
White, Nik, 91
Wildlife safety tips, 167
Williams, Robin, 84
Wolden, Freida, 51
Work. See also Volunteerism
balancing, 194–95
full-time work, 172–86, 245
ideas for, 172–86, 191
Internet connections for, 186–90
managing expectations of, 184–86
part-time work, 172–86
remote working, 20–23, 30, 91, 137, 141, 172–77, 185, 195, 247
seasonal work, 180–81
self-employment, 144–45, 165, 176–86, 191
work camping, 20–21, 135, 137, 140–45, 165, 178–80, 185
World Wide Opportunities on Organic Farms (WWOOFing), 181

IMAGE CREDITS